Splunk Best Prac

Design, implement, and publish custom Splunk applications by following best practices

Travis Marlette

BIRMINGHAM - MUMBAI

Splunk Best Practices

First published: September 2016

Production reference: 1150916

Published by Packt Publishing Ltd.

Livery Place

35 Livery Street

Birmingham B3 2PB, UK.

ISBN 978-1-78528-139-6

www.packtpub.com

Credits

Author

Travis Marlette

Reviewer

Chris Ladd

Commissioning Editor

Veena Pagare

Acquisition Editor

Tushar Gupta

Content Development Editor

Prashanth G Rao

Technical Editor

Murtaza Tinwala

Copy Editor

Safis Editing

Project Coordinator

Ulhas Kambali

Proofreader

Safis Editing

Indexer

Tejal Daruwale Soni

Production Coordinator

Melwyn Dsa

Cover Work

Melwyn Dsa

About the Author

Travis Marlette has been working with Splunk since Splunk 4.0, and has over 7 years of statistical and analytical experience leveraging both Splunk and other technologies. He cut his teeth in the securities and equities division of the finance industry, routing stock market data and performing transactional analysis on stock market trading, as well as reporting security metrics for SEC and other federal audits.

His specialty is in IT operational intelligence, which consists of the lions share of many major companies. Being able to report on security, system-specific, and propriety application metrics is always a challenge for any company and with the increase of IT in the modern day, having a specialist like this will become more and more prominent.

Working in finance, Travis has experience of working to integrate Splunk with some of the newest and most complex technologies, such as:

- SAS
- HIVE
- TerraData (Data Warehouse)
- Oozie
- EMC (Xtreme IO)
- Datameer
- ZFS
- Compass
- Cisco (Security/Network)
- Platfora
- Juniper (Security and Network)
- IBM Web Sphere
- Cisco Call Manager
- Java Management Systems (JVM)
- Cisco UCS
- IBM MQ Series
- FireEye
- Microsoft Active Directory
- Snort
- Microsoft Exchange

- F5
- Microsoft – OS
- MapR (Hadoop)
- Microsoft SQL
- YARN (Hadoop)
- Microsoft SCOM
- NoSQL
- Linux (Red Hat / Cent OS)
- Oracle
- MySQL
- Nagios
- LDAP
- TACACS+
- ADS
- Kerberos
- Gigamon
- Telecom Inventory Management
- Riverbed Suite
- Endace
- Service Now
- JIRA
- Confluence

Travis is has been certified for a series of Microsoft, Juniper, Cisco, Splunk, and network security certifications. His knowledge and experience is truly his most valued currency, and this is demonstrated by every organization that has worked with him to reach their goals.

He has worked with Splunk installations that ingest 80 to 150 GB daily, as well as 6 TB daily, and provided value with each of the installations he's created to the companies that he's worked with. In addition he also knows when a project sponsor or manager requires more information about Splunk and helps them understand what Splunk is, and how it can best bring value to their organization without over-committing.

According to Travis, "Splunk is not a 'crystal ball'that's made of unicorn tears, and bottled rainbows, granting wishes and immediate gratification to the person who possesses it. It's an IT platform that requires good resources supporting it, and is limited only by the knowledge and imagination of those resources". With the right resources, that's a good limitation for a company to have.

Splunk acts as a 'Rosetta Stone' of sorts for machines. It takes thousands of machines, speaking totally different languages all at the same time, and translates that into something a human can understand. This by itself, is powerful.

His passion for innovating new solutions and overcoming challenges leveraging Splunk and other data science tools have been exercised and visualized every day each of his roles. Those roles are cross industry, ranging from Bank of New York and Barclay's Capital, to the Federal Government. Thus far, he and the teams he has worked with have taken each of these organizations further than they have ever been on their Splunk journey. While he continues to bring visibility, add value, consolidate tools, share work, perform predictions, and implement cost savings, he is also are often mentioned as the most resourceful, reliable, and goofy person in the organization. Travis says "A new Splunk implementation is like asking your older brother to turn on a fire hose so you can get a drink of water. Once it's on, just remember to breathe."

About the Reviewer

Chris Ladd is a staff sales engineer at Splunk. He has been with Splunk for three years and has been a sales engineer for more than a decade. He has earned degrees from Southwestern University and the University of Houston. He resides in Chicago.

www.PacktPub.com

eBooks, discount offers, and more

Did you know that Packt offers eBook versions of every book published, with PDF and ePub files available? You can upgrade to the eBook version at www.PacktPub.com and as a print book customer, you are entitled to a discount on the eBook copy. Get in touch with us at customercare@packtpub.com for more details.

At www.PacktPub.com, you can also read a collection of free technical articles, sign up for a range of free newsletters and receive exclusive discounts and offers on Packt books and eBooks.

https://www2.packtpub.com/books/subscription/packtlib

Do you need instant solutions to your IT questions? PacktLib is Packt's online digital book library. Here, you can search, access, and read Packt's entire library of books.

Why subscribe?

- Fully searchable across every book published by Packt
- Copy and paste, print, and bookmark content
- On demand and accessible via a web browser

Table of Contents

Preface

Within the working world of technology, there are hundreds of thousands of different applications, all (usually) logging in different formats. As a *Splunk expert*, our job is make all those logs speak human, which is often the impossible task. With third-party applications that provide support, sometimes log formatting is out of our control. Take, for instance, Cisco or Juniper, or any other leading leading manufacturer.

These devices submit structured data,specific to the manufacturer. There are also applications that we have more influence on, which are usually custom applications built for a specific purpose by the development staff of your organization. These are usually referred to as 'Proprietary applications' or 'in-house' or 'home grown' all of which mean the same thing.

The logs I am referencing belong to proprietary in-house (a.k.a. *home grown*) applications that are often part of the middleware, and usually control some of the most mission critical services an organization can provide.

Proprietary applications can be written in anything, but logging is usually left up to the developers for troubleshooting, and up until now the process of manually scraping log files to troubleshoot quality assurance issues and system outages has been very specific. I mean that usually, the developer(s) are the only people that truly understand what those log messages mean.

That being said, developers often write their logs in a way that they can understand them, because ultimately it will be them doing the troubleshooting / code fixing when something severe breaks.

As an IT community, we haven't really started taking a look at the *way* we log things, but instead we have tried to limit the confusion to developers, and then have them help other SMEs that provide operational support, understand what is actually happening.

This method has been successful, but time consuming, and the true value of any SME is reducing any systems MTTR, and increasing uptime. With any system, the more transactions processed means the larger the scale of a system, which after about 20 machines, troubleshooting begins to get more complex, and time consuming with a manual process.

The goal of this book is to give you some techniques to build a bridge in your organization. We will assume you have a base understanding of what Splunk does, so that we can provide a few tools to make your day to day life easier with Splunk and not get bogged down in the vast array of SDK's and matching languages, and API's. These tools range from intermediate to expert levels. My hope is that at least one person can take at least one concept from this book, to make their lives easier.

What this book covers

Chapter 1, *Application Logging*, discusses where the application data comes from, and how that data gets into Splunk, and how it reacts to the data. You will develop applications, or scripts, and also learn how to adjust Splunk to handle some non-standardized logging. Splunk is as turnkey, as the data you put it into it. This means, if you have a 20-year-old application that logs unstructured data in debug mode only, your Splunk instance will not be a turnkey. With a system such a Splunk, we can quote some data science experts in saying "*garbage in, garbage out*".

Chapter 2, *Data Inputs*, discusses how to move on to understanding what kinds of data input Splunk uses in order to get data inputs. We see how to enable Splunk to use the methods which they have developed in data inputs. Finally, you will get a brief introduction to the data inputs for Splunk.

Chapter 3, *Data Scrubbing*, discusses how to format all incoming data to a Splunk, friendly format, pre-indexing in order to ease search querying, and knowledge management going forward.

Chapter 4, *Knowledge management*, explains some techniques of managing the incoming data to your Splunk indexers, some basics of how to leverage those knowledge objects to enhance performance when searching, as well as the pros and cons of pre and post field extraction.

Chapter 5, *Alerting*, discusses the growing importance of Splunk alerting, and the different levels of doing so. In the current corporate environment, intelligent alerting, and alert 'noise' reduction are becoming more important due to machine sprawl, both horizontally and vertically. Later, we will discuss how to create intelligent alerts, manage them effectively, and also some methods of 'self-healing' that I've used in the past and the successes and consequences of such methods in order to assist in setting expectations.

Chapter 6, *Searching and Reporting*, will talk about the anatomy of a search, and then some key techniques that help in real-world scenarios. Many people understand search syntax, however to use it effectively, (a.k.a to become a search ninja) is something much more evasive and continuous. We will also see real world use-cases in order to get the point across such as, merging two datasets at search time, and making the result set of a two searches match each other in time.

Chapter 7, *Form-Based Dashboards*, discusses how to create form based dashboards leveraging foo variables as selectors to appropriately pass information to another search, or another dashboard and also, we see how to create an effective *drill-down* effect.

Chapter 8, *Search optimization*, shows how to optimize the dashboards to increase performance. This ultimately effects how quickly dashboards load results. We do that by adjusting search queries, leverage summary indexes, the KV Store, accelerated searches, and data models to name a few.

Chapter 9, *App Creation and Consolidation*, discusses how to take a series of apps from Splunkbase, as well as any dashboard that is user created, and put them into a Splunk app for ease of use. We also talk about how to adjust the navigation XML to ease user navigation of such an app.

Chapter 10, *Advanced Data Routing*, discusses something that is becoming more common place in an enterprise. As many people are using big data platforms like Splunk to move data around their network things such as firewalls and data stream loss, sourcetype renaming by environment can become administratively expensive.

What you need for this book

You will need at least a distributed deployment of an on prem installation of Splunk for this book, collecting both Linux and Windows information, and a heavy forwarder as well. We will use all of these pieces to show you techniques to add value.

Who this book is for

This book is for administrators, developers, and search ninjas who have been using Splunk for some time. A comprehensive coverage makes this book great for Splunk veterans and newbies alike.

Conventions

In this book, you will find a number of text styles that distinguish between different kinds of information. Here are some examples of these styles and an explanation of their meaning.

Code words in text, database table names, folder names, filenames, file extensions, pathnames, dummy URLs, user input, and Twitter handles are shown as follows: "For instance, in Cisco log files there is a `src_ip` field."

A block of code is set as follows:

```
[mySourcetype]
REPORT-fields = myLinuxScript_fields
```

When we wish to draw your attention to a particular part of a code block, the relevant lines or items are set in bold:

```
[myUnstructured]
DATETIME_CONFIG =
NO_BINARY_CHECK = true
category = Custom
pulldown_type = true
```

Any command-line input or output is written as follows:

```
ssh -v -p 8089 mydeploymentserver.com
```

New terms and **important words** are shown in bold. Words that you see on the screen, for example, in menus or dialog boxes, appear in the text like this: "The most common messages we see are things like **unauthorized login attempt <user>** or **Connection Timed out to <ip address>**."

Warnings or important notes appear in a box like this.

Tips and tricks appear like this.

Reader feedback

Feedback from our readers is always welcome. Let us know what you think about this book—what you liked or disliked. Reader feedback is important for us as it helps us develop titles that you will really get the most out of.

To send us general feedback, simply e-mail feedback@packtpub.com, and mention the book's title in the subject of your message.

If there is a topic that you have expertise in and you are interested in either writing or contributing to a book, see our author guide at www.packtpub.com/authors.

Customer support

Now that you are the proud owner of a Packt book, we have a number of things to help you to get the most from your purchase.

Downloading the example code

You can download the example code files for this book from your account at http://www.packtpub.com. If you purchased this book elsewhere, you can visit http://www.packtpub.com/support and register to have the files e-mailed directly to you.

You can download the code files by following these steps:

1. Log in or register to our website using your e-mail address and password.
2. Hover the mouse pointer on the **SUPPORT** tab at the top.
3. Click on **Code Downloads & Errata**.
4. Enter the name of the book in the **Search** box.
5. Select the book for which you're looking to download the code files.
6. Choose from the drop-down menu where you purchased this book from.
7. Click on **Code Download**.

You can also download the code files by clicking on the **Code Files** button on the book's webpage at the Packt Publishing website. This page can be accessed by entering the book's name in the **Search** box. Please note that you need to be logged in to your Packt account.

Once the file is downloaded, please make sure that you unzip or extract the folder using the latest version of:

- WinRAR / 7-Zip for Windows
- Zipeg / iZip / UnRarX for Mac
- 7-Zip / PeaZip for Linux

The code bundle for the book is also hosted on GitHub at `https://github.com/PacktPubl ishing/Splunk-Best-Practices`. We also have other code bundles from our rich catalog of books and videos available at `https://github.com/PacktPublishing/`. Check them out!

Downloading the color images of this book

We also provide you with a PDF file that has color images of the screenshots/diagrams used in this book. The color images will help you better understand the changes in the output. You can download this file from `https://www.packtpub.com/sites/default/files/down loads/SplunkBestPractices_ColorImages.pdf`.

Errata

Although we have taken every care to ensure the accuracy of our content, mistakes do happen. If you find a mistake in one of our books—maybe a mistake in the text or the code—we would be grateful if you could report this to us. By doing so, you can save other readers from frustration and help us improve subsequent versions of this book. If you find any errata, please report them by visiting `http://www.packtpub.com/submit-errata`, selecting your book, clicking on the **Errata Submission Form** link, and entering the details of your errata. Once your errata are verified, your submission will be accepted and the errata will be uploaded to our website or added to any list of existing errata under the Errata section of that title.

To view the previously submitted errata, go to `https://www.packtpub.com/books/conten t/support` and enter the name of the book in the search field. The required information will appear under the **Errata** section.

Piracy

Piracy of copyrighted material on the Internet is an ongoing problem across all media. At Packt, we take the protection of our copyright and licenses very seriously. If you come across any illegal copies of our works in any form on the Internet, please provide us with the location address or website name immediately so that we can pursue a remedy.

Please contact us at `copyright@packtpub.com` with a link to the suspected pirated material.

We appreciate your help in protecting our authors and our ability to bring you valuable content.

Questions

If you have a problem with any aspect of this book, you can contact us at `questions@packtpub.com`, and we will do our best to address the problem.

1
Application Logging

Within the working world of technology, there are hundreds of thousands of different applications, all (usually) logging in different formats. As *Splunk experts*, our job is make all those logs speak human, which is often an impossible task. With third-party applications that provide support, sometimes log formatting is out of our control. Take for instance, Cisco or Juniper, or any other leading application manufacturer. We won't be discussing these kinds of logs in this chapter, but we'll discuss the logs that we do have some control over.

The logs I am referencing belong to proprietary in-house (also known as "home grown") applications that are often part of middleware, and usually they control some of the most mission-critical services an organization can provide.

Proprietary applications can be written in any language. However, logging is usually left up to the developers for troubleshooting and up until now the process of manually scraping log files to troubleshoot quality assurance issues and system outages has been very specific. I mean that usually, the developer(s) are the only people that truly understand what those log messages mean.

That being said, oftentimes developers write their logs in a way that they can understand them, because ultimately it will be them doing the troubleshooting/code fixing when something breaks severely.

As an IT community, we haven't really started looking at the way we log things, but instead we have tried to limit the confusion to developers, and then have them help other SME's that provide operational support to understand what is actually happening.

This method is successful, however, it is slow, and the true value of any SME is reducing any system's MTTR, and increasing uptime.

With any system, the more transactions processed means the larger the scale of the system, which means that, after about 20 machines, troubleshooting begins to get more complex and time consuming with a manual process.

This is where something like Splunk can be extremely valuable. However, Splunk is only as good as the information that comes into it.

I will say this phrase for the people who haven't heard it yet; *"garbage in... garbage out"*

There are some ways to turn proprietary logging into a powerful tool, and I have personally seen the value of these kinds of logs. After formatting them for Splunk, they turn into a huge asset in an organization's software life cycle.

I'm not here to tell you this is easy, but I am here to give you some good practices about how to format proprietary logs.

To do that I'll start by helping you appreciate a very silent and critical piece of the application stack.

To developers, a logging mechanism is a very important part of the stack, and the log itself is mission critical. What we haven't spent much time thinking about before log analyzers, is how to make log events/messages/exceptions more *machine friendly* so that we can socialize the information in a system like Splunk, and start to bridge the knowledge gap between development and operations.

The nicer we format the logs, the faster Splunk can reveal the information about our systems, saving everyone time and headaches.

In this chapter we are briefly going to look at the following topics:

- Log messengers
- Logging formats
- Correlation IDs and why they help
- When to place correlation ID in a log

Loggers

Here I will give some very high level information on loggers. My intention is not to recommend logging tools, but simply to raise awareness of their existence for those that are not in development, and allow for independent research into what they do. With the right developer, and the right Splunker, the logger turns into something immensely valuable to an organization.

There is an array of different loggers in the IT universe, and I'm only going to touch on a couple of them here. Keep in mind that I only reference these due to the ease of development I've seen from personal experience, and experiences do vary.

I'm only going to touch on three loggers and then move on to formatting, as there are tons of logging mechanisms and the preference truly depends on the developer.

Anatomy of a log

I'm going to be taking some very broad strokes with the following explanations in order to familiarize you, the Splunk administrator, with the development version of 'the logger'. Each language has its own versions of 'the logger' which is really only a function written in that software language that writes application relevant messages to a log file. If you would like to learn more information, please either seek out a developer to help you understand the logic better or acquire some education on how to develop and log in independent study.

There are some pretty basic components to logging that we need to understand to learn which type of data we are looking at. I'll start with the four most common ones:

- **Log events**: This is the entirety of the message we see within a log, often starting with a timestamp. The event itself contains all other aspects of application behavior such as fields, exceptions, messages, and so on… think of this as the "container" if you will, for information.
- **Messages**: These are often made by the developer of the application and provide some human insight into what's actually happening within an application. The most common messages we see are things like **unauthorized login attempt <user>** or **Connection Timed out to <ip address>**.
- **Message Fields**: These are the pieces of information that give us the *who, where,* and *when* types of information for the application's actions. They are handed to the logger by the application itself as it either attempts or completes an activity. For instance, in the log event below, the highlighted pieces are what would be fields, and often those that people look for when troubleshooting:

```
"2/19/2011 6:17:46 AM Using 'xplog70.dll' version
'2009.100.1600' to execute extended store procedure
'xp_common_1' operation failed to connect to 'DB_XCUTE_STOR'"
```

- **Exceptions**: These are the uncommon but very important pieces of the log. They are usually only written when something goes wrong, and offer developer insight into the root cause at the application layer. They are usually only printed when an error occurs, and are used for debugging.

  These exceptions can print a huge amount of information into the log depending on the developer and the framework. The format itself is not easy and in some cases is not even possible for a developer to manage.

Log4*

This is an open source logger that is often used in middleware applications.

Pantheios

This is a logger popularly used for Linux, and popular for its performance and multi-threaded handling of logging. Commonly, Pantheios is used for C/C++ applications, but it works with a multitude of frameworks.

Logging – logging facility for Python

This is a logger specifically for Python, and since Python is becoming more and more popular, this is a very common package used to log Python scripts and applications.

Each one of these loggers has their own way of logging, and the value is determined by the application developer. If there is no standardized logging, then one can imagine the confusion this can bring to troubleshooting.

Example of a structured log

This is an example of a Java exception in a structured log format:

```
*** BASIC REND RENDERING   org.jdesktop.wonderland.modules.orb.client.cell.OrbCellRenderer@76fe98
*** BASIC REND VISIBLE   org.jdesktop.wonderland.modules.orb.client.cell.OrbCellRenderer@76fe9831
Jul 8, 2009 6:15:05 PM org.jdesktop.wonderland.modules.appbase.client.swing.WindowSwing requestI
WARNING: Focus request for embedded component rejected.
Jul 8, 2009 6:15:06 PM org.jdesktop.wonderland.modules.appbase.client.swing.WindowSwing$1 run
WARNING: Focus request for main canvas rejected.
Jul 8, 2009 6:15:19 PM com.sun.sgs.impl.io.CompleteMessageFilter processReceiveBuffer
WARNING: Exception in message disptach; dropping message
java.lang.NullPointerException
        at org.jdesktop.wonderland.modules.orb.client.cell.OrbMessageHandler.done(OrbMessageHand
        at org.jdesktop.wonderland.modules.orb.client.cell.OrbMessageHandler.processMessage(Orb
        at org.jdesktop.wonderland.modules.orb.client.cell.OrbMessageHandler$1.messageReceived(
        at org.jdesktop.wonderland.client.cell.ChannelComponent.deliverMessage(ChannelComponent.
        at org.jdesktop.wonderland.client.cell.ChannelComponent.messageReceived(ChannelComponent
        at org.jdesktop.wonderland.client.cell.CellChannelConnection.handleMessage(CellChannelCo
        at org.jdesktop.wonderland.client.comms.BaseConnection.messageReceived(BaseConnection.j
        at org.jdesktop.wonderland.client.comms.WonderlandSessionImpl$ClientRecord.handleMessage
        at org.jdesktop.wonderland.client.comms.WonderlandSessionImpl.fireSessionMessageReceived
        at org.jdesktop.wonderland.client.comms.WonderlandSessionImpl$WonderlandClientListener$
        at com.sun.sgs.client.simple.SimpleClient$SimpleClientChannel.receivedMessage(SimpleClie
        at com.sun.sgs.client.simple.SimpleClient$SimpleClientConnectionListener.handleChannelMe
        at com.sun.sgs.client.simple.SimpleClient$SimpleClientConnectionListener.handleApplicati
        at com.sun.sgs.client.simple.SimpleClient$SimpleClientConnectionListener.receivedMessage
        at com.sun.sgs.impl.client.simple.SimpleClientConnection.bytesReceived(SimpleClientConne
        at com.sun.sgs.impl.io.SocketConnection.filteredMessageReceived(SocketConnection.java:1
        at com.sun.sgs.impl.io.CompleteMessageFilter.processReceiveBuffer(CompleteMessageFilter
        at com.sun.sgs.impl.io.CompleteMessageFilter.filterReceive(CompleteMessageFilter.java:1
        at com.sun.sgs.impl.io.SocketConnectionListener.messageReceived(SocketConnectionListener
        at org.apache.mina.common.support.AbstractIoFilterChain$TailFilter.messageReceived(Abst
        at org.apache.mina.common.support.AbstractIoFilterChain.callNextMessageReceived(Abstract
        at org.apache.mina.common.support.AbstractIoFilterChain.access$1100(AbstractIoFilterCha
        at org.apache.mina.common.support.AbstractIoFilterChain$EntryImpl$1.messageReceived(Abs
        at org.apache.mina.filter.executor.ExecutorFilter.processEvent(ExecutorFilter.java:247)
        at org.apache.mina.filter.executor.ExecutorFilter$ProcessEventsRunnable.run(ExecutorFil
        at java.util.concurrent.ThreadPoolExecutor$Worker.runTask(ThreadPoolExecutor.java:885)
        at java.util.concurrent.ThreadPoolExecutor$Worker.run(ThreadPoolExecutor.java:907)
        at java.lang.Thread.run(Thread.java:637)
Jul 8, 2009 6:15:19 PM org.jdesktop.wonderland.client.cell.CellCacheBasicImpl unloadCell
WARNING: -------> UNLOADING CELL 50
Jul 8, 2009 6:15:19 PM org.jdesktop.wonderland.client.cell.CellCacheBasicImpl setCellStatus
FINE: Set status of cell 50 to DISK
*** BASIC REND RENDERING   org.jdesktop.wonderland.modules.orb.client.cell.OrbCellRenderer@5321d
*** BASIC REND ACTIVE   org.jdesktop.wonderland.modules.orb.client.cell.OrbCellRenderer@5321d174
*** BASIC REND INACTIVE   org.jdesktop.wonderland.modules.orb.client.cell.OrbCellRenderer@5321d1
*** BASIC REND DISK   org.jdesktop.wonderland.modules.orb.client.cell.OrbCellRenderer@5321d174
Jul 8, 2009 6:15:19 PM org.jdesktop.wonderland.client.cell.CellCacheBasicImpl unloadCell
WARNING: -------> UNLOADING ROOT CELL 50
```

Log format – null pointer exception

When Java prints an exception, it will be displayed in the format as shown in the preceding screenshot, and a developer doesn't control what that format is. They can control some aspects about what is included within an exception, though the arrangement of the characters and how it's written is done by the Java framework itself.

I mention this last part in order to help operational people understand where the control of a developer sometimes ends. My own personal experience has taught me that attempting to change a format that is handled within the framework itself is an attempt at futility. Pick your battles, right? As a Splunker, you can save yourself headaches on this kind of thing.

Data types

There are generally two formats that Splunkers will need to categorize to weigh the amount of effort that goes into bringing the data to a dashboard:

- **Structured data**: These are usually logs for Apache, IIS, Windows events, Cisco, and some other manufacturers.
- **Unstructured data**: This type of logging usually comes from a proprietary application where each message can be printed differently in different operations and the event itself can span multiple lines with no definitive event start, or event end, or both. Often, this is the bulk of our data.

Structured data – best practices

In the land of unicorn tears, money trees, and elven magic, IT logs come in the same format, no matter what the platform, and every engineer lives happily ever after.

In our earthly reality, IT logs come in millions of proprietary formats, some structured and others unstructured, waiting to blind the IT engineer with confusion and bewilderment at a moment's notice and suck the very will to continue on their path to problem resolution out of them every day.

As Splunk experts, there are some ways that we can work with our developers in order to ease the process of bringing value to people through machine logs, one of which is to *standardize* on a log format across platforms. This in effect is creating a structured logging format.

Now when I say "cross-platform" and "standardize", I'm focusing on the in-house platform logs that are within your Splunk indexes and controlled by your in-house development staff right now. We can't affect the way a framework like Java, .NET, Windows, or Cisco log their information, so let's focus on what we can potentially improve. For the rest, we will have to create some Splunk logic to do what's called **data normalization**. Data normalization is the process of making the field *user* equal *user* across your entire first, second, and third-party systems. For instance, in Cisco log files there is a `src_ip` field. However, in the Juniper world, there is the `source_address` field. Data normalization is the act of making it so that you can reference a source IP address with a single field name across multiple data sets. In our example lets say `source_ip` represents both the `src_ip` field from Cisco, and the `source_address` from Juniper.

Log events

There are a few ways we can standardize on log event formats, and some systems already have these kinds of logging in place. The most Splunk-friendly ways are going to be either key=value pairs, or delimited values, JSON, or XML. I can tell you, through experience, that the easiest way to get Splunk to auto recognize the fields in a log is to use `key=value` pairs when writing to a log.

Let me give a couple examples of the structured data formats so you at least know what the data looks like:

```
17/10/2014   { [-]
16:46:30.000    bytes: 2877
                clientip:
                duration: 355526
                host: www.ezix.org
                message:           - - [17/Oct/2014:16:46:30 +0200] "GET /project/wiki/AccessJSON HTTP/1.1"
            200 2877
                method: GET
                pname: httpd
                port: 443
                protocol: HTTP/1.1
                referer:
                request: /project/wiki/AccessJSON
                ssl: 1
                sslcipher: ECDHE-RSA-AES128-GCM-SHA256
                sslexport: false
                sslkeysize: 128
                sslprotocol: TLSv1.2
                sslvirtualhost:
                status: 200
                tags: [ [+]
                ]
                time: 2014-10-17T16:46:30+0200
                urlpath: /project/wiki/AccessJSON
                urlquery: null
                user: -
                useragent: Mozilla/5.0 (X11; Linux x86_64; rv:32.0) Gecko/20100101 Firefox/32.0
                virtualhost: www.ezix.org
            }
            Show as raw text
            host =         host = www.ezix.org    source = /var/log/httpd/access.json    sourcetype = json-2    ssl = 1
```

JSON Logging format (this is how Splunk parses JSON logs)

Common Log Format

You can find some information about Common Log Format at: https://en.wikipedia.org /wiki/Common_Log_Format.

The following dataset is very easy to parse within Splunk.

```
127.0.0.1 user-identifier frank [10/Oct/2000:13:55:36 -0700] "GET
/apache_pb.gif HTTP/1.0" 200 2326
```

In this next example, we will learn how:

This is a delimited value format, and for ease we will be looking at web logs.

In the following image, we see that each log event is structured with `<value1>`, `<value2>`, and so on. This is a comma delimited log format that Splunk is quite happy with receiving, and pulling information out of:

```
198.70.37.65, -, 3/31/96, 2:12:09, W3SVC, PAOLO, 198.70.37.65, 2814, 167, 3636, 200, 0, GET, /index.htm, -,
198.70.37.65, -, 3/31/96, 2:12:11, W3SVC, PAOLO, 198.70.37.65, 921, 214, 2360, 200, 0, GET, /Graphics/extra.jpg, -,
198.70.37.65, -, 3/31/96, 2:12:11, W3SVC, PAOLO, 198.70.37.65, 701, 215, 4108, 200, 0, GET, /graphics/events.gif, -,
198.70.37.65, -, 3/31/96, 2:12:11, W3SVC, PAOLO, 198.70.37.65, 871, 216, 2106, 200, 0, GET, /Graphics/WWWSTAT.JPG, -,
198.70.37.65, -, 3/31/96, 2:12:11, W3SVC, PAOLO, 198.70.37.65, 90, 215, 2411, 200, 0, GET, /graphics/public.jpg, -,
198.70.37.65, -, 3/31/96, 2:12:11, W3SVC, PAOLO, 198.70.37.65, 1222, 216, 9335, 200, 0, GET, /graphics/wintugi.jpg, -,
198.70.37.65, -, 3/31/96, 2:12:13, W3SVC, PAOLO, 198.70.37.65, 2113, 216, 3993, 200, 0, GET, /graphics/members.gif, -,
198.70.37.65, -, 3/31/96, 2:12:13, W3SVC, PAOLO, 198.70.37.65, 1742, 216, 2528, 200, 0, GET, /graphics/sponsor.jpg, -,
198.70.37.65, -, 3/31/96, 2:12:13, W3SVC, PAOLO, 198.70.37.65, 2594, 213, 3993, 200, 0, GET, /graphics/NTRC.gif, -,
198.70.37.65, -, 3/31/96, 2:12:13, W3SVC, PAOLO, 198.70.37.65, 2694, 213, 3138, 200, 0, GET, /graphics/join.jpg, -,
198.70.37.65, -, 3/31/96, 2:12:14, W3SVC, PAOLO, 198.70.37.65, 901, 215, 4049, 200, 0, GET, /graphics/roster.gif, -,
198.70.37.65, -, 3/31/96, 2:12:18, W3SVC, PAOLO, 198.70.37.65, 4797, 249, 72, 200, 0, GET, /index.htm, -,
```

Innately, Splunk will understand the structure of an IIS type of log event. However, in some cases it's up to the Splunk engineer to tell Splunk the field names, and the order of each of these events. This is basically event and field extraction, and it's also how we start organizing and managing the value of a dataset.

In this example there are a couple of ways of extracting knowledge from these events, and I will give both the automatic way and the manual way.

Architectural Notes
In the following example the architecture being used is a distributed search deployment, with one search head and one indexer.

Automatic Delimited Value Extraction (IIS/Apache) – best practice

This type of value extraction is performed automatically by the back end Splunk programming. It looks for specific sourcetypes and data structures and extracts fields from them as long as you send data from each forwarder appropriately. For instance, IIS or apache logs.

In order to forward data appropriately, you'll need to:

1. Tell each forwarder on your IIS/Apache Machines to send data to the following source types (your choice of index):
   - access_combined – Apache
   - IIS – IIS

2. Make sure your Apache/IIS logs have the fields enabled for logging that Splunk is expecting (for more insight on this please see the Splunk documentation`https://docs.splunk.com/Documentation`.

After that, just run a search for `index=<my_index> sourcetype=iis` and if your forwarders/indexers are sending and receiving data properly, you should see data and the fields will be extracted in the **Interesting Fields** panel in Splunk. Voila, you're done!

This IIS/Apache automatic field extraction is available by default in Splunk which makes it nice for these data sets. If your source types are not named in this fashion, the extractions will not work for you out of the box as field extraction happens primarily at the source type level. If you would like to see all of the configuration for the IIS dataset, go to the following locations and look at the stanza:

`$PLUNK_HOME/etc/system/default/props.conf-[iis]`, then take a look at the documentation if you want to learn more about the settings.

IIS data in Splunk should look something like this:

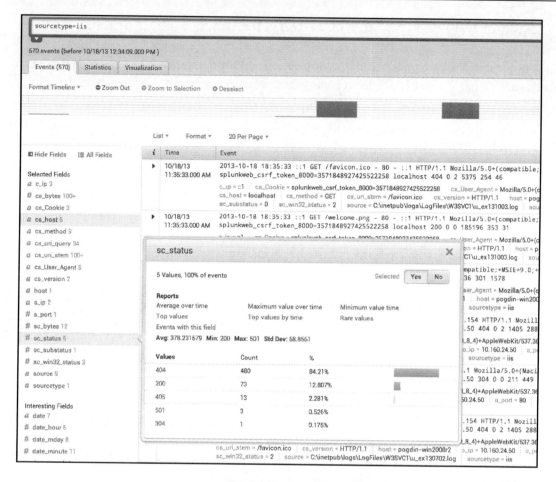

IIS data in Splunk with sc_status

Notice all of the fields that are being extracted under **Interesting Fields**.

Splunk has only extracted a handful of log types, such as IIS/Apache logs, by default and cannot be leveraged on other datasets. Many of the other datasets are extracted using either an app from Splunkbase or the manual method. For a full list of datasets Splunk has programmed for automatic field extraction, please visit `http://www.splunk.com/`.

The whole goal of this chapter is to achieve this type of knowledge extraction most efficiently, as all of this is very helpful once we start building searches in Splunk. The most effective way to do this is by literally starting at the log format itself.

Manual Delimited Value Extraction with REGEX

I will not be getting into how to work with **REGEX** in this book at all. I can only suggest that if you're a Splunk admin and you're not fluent with it… learn it quickly. RegExr (`http://regexr.com/`) is a fantastic tool for learning this language or you can also visit `https://regex11.com/`. Below is an image of `regexr.com/v1` (the old version of the tool):

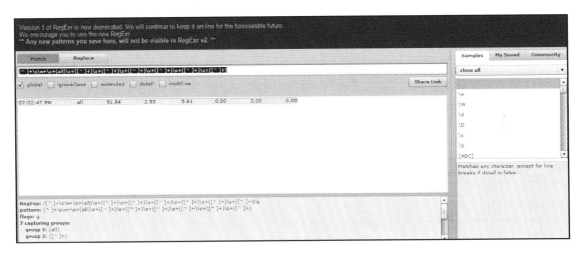

This technique can be used on any structured log data that is delimited, that Splunk itself doesn't have knowledge extraction of by default.

For this we are going to use the same type of structured data, but let's say that Splunk isn't extracting the data fields, though the data is already being input into Splunk. The data's source is a bash script that was created by a Linux system admin that required specifics on their set of machines.

Step 1 – field mapping – best practice

This is as easy as speaking to the expert whose system the data belongs to.

In this example, the bash scripts output that is coming into Splunk is in a structured but unlabeled format:

07:02:47 PM	all	91.84	2.55	5.61	0.00	0.00	0.00
07:02:49 PM	all	29.74	49.74	7.69	0.00	0.00	12.82
07:02:51 PM	all	0.50	0.00	1.51	0.00	0.00	97.99
07:02:53 PM	all	5.05	0.00	15.15	0.00	0.00	79.80
07:02:55 PM	all	19.50	0.00	34.50	4.00	0.00	42.00
07:02:57 PM	all	8.59	0.00	10.10	0.00	0.00	81.31

If a general Splunk admin was to look at this data, it would appear to mean something, but it wouldn't be clear as to what. The person who does have clarity is the person who wrote the script. Our job as Splunk experts is often to go find out what this information means. I call this *the process of discovery*.

We can see a timestamp here, but after that, it's a series of information that makes no sense. The only thing we know for sure is that something is being printed at 2 second intervals and there are multiple values.

When we go to our SME, we need to ask him how he structured the data output that is being printed. Writing that information down will give us the field mappings we are looking for so we can structure this.

When we ask our SME, they will give us an answer that looks like this:

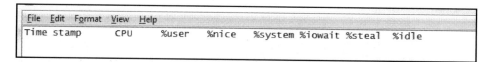

This is our field map, so now all we need to do is tell Splunk how to extract these characters being delimited by a space.

This is a quick and easy prop/`transforms.conf` setting.

Step 2 – adding the field map to structure the data (props/transforms)

For this example, we will just be using the standard search app, so we are going to adjust the settings there. We will be using REGEX to extract the fields and then standard bash variables to map each REGEX group to its field.

I'm going to add the following stanza to the `transforms.conf` in `$SPLUNK_HOME/etc/apps/search/local/transforms.conf`:

```
[myLinuxScript_fields]
REGEX = [^ ]+\s\w+\s+(all)\s+([^ ]+)\s+([^ ]+)\s+([^ ]+)\s+([^ ]+)\s+([^
]+)\s+([^ ]+)

FORMAT = cpu::$1 pctUser::$2 pctNice::$3 pctSys::$4 pctIOwait::$5
pctSteal::$6 pctIdle::$7
```

This REGEX gives Splunk the appropriate capture groups you want to label. These capture groups are signified by the parenthesis in the REGEX above.

I'm also going to call that transform in `$SPLUNK_HOME/etc/apps/search/local/props.conf` for my source type. We need this reference in order to extract our fields:

```
[mySourcetype]
REPORT-fields = myLinuxScript_fields
```

Then we restart the Splunk service on the search head and we should see our new fields.

In the above transform, each REGEX capture group, represented by `()`, and anything in between them is mapped to a numerical variable. However, the capture groups must be contiguous and sequential. You can't have 10 capture groups and expect $1 to be the 5th group captured. $1 maps to capture group 1, $2 to capture group 2, and so on.

This is the data input from line 1 of the preceding image, with the method explained:

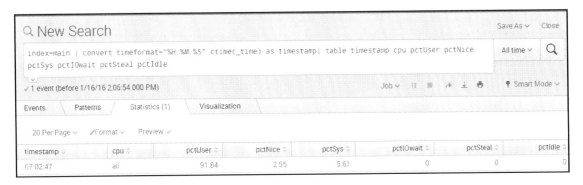

Use correlation IDs– best practice

If you're developing an application in the world of structured data and mature logging, there are all kinds of lovely fields that can be used to bring value to our data with Splunk. One of the most valuable fields I've found in the development world that helps Splunk track a transaction end-to-end through a system is a correlation ID.

This is a field that is attached to the initial action of a user on a frontend, and that field value is passed down through the stack from frontend to middleware, to database call and back again during each action or transaction that is committed. This field is usually a uniquely generated GUID that, to Splunk, has huge potential.

Without something like a correlation ID, it's much more difficult to track activities from end-to-end, because many transactions within an application are looked at based on timestamp when troubleshooting. This little field will make your life profoundly easier if used properly with Splunk.

Some systems already have correlation IDs, such as SharePoint logging. However, many do not. If you're a developer of middleware and you're reading this, please use this field, as it makes mining for your data a lot easier.

This is an example of a SharePoint log with a correlation ID:

Time	Thread	Product	Category	EventID	Level	Correlation	Message
01/29/2011 14:...	0x2A50	Share...	Monito...	b4ly	High	a6ea7f59-7b54-46f8-9e68-5be81172704c	Leaving Monitored Scope (Creating Web BI). Executio
01/29/2011 14:...	0x2A50	Share...	General	85m6	Medium	a6ea7f59-7b54-46f8-9e68-5be81172704c	Applying web template 'BICenterSite#0' on web url 'htt
01/29/2011 14:...	0x2A50	Share...	General	85m7	Medium	a6ea7f59-7b54-46f8-9e68-5be81172704c	Actual web template to apply to Url 'http://latide6510-
01/29/2011 14:...	0x2A50	Share...	General	72h7	Medium	a6ea7f59-7b54-46f8-9e68-5be81172704c	Applying template "BICenterSite#0" to web at URL "h
01/29/2011 14:...	0x2A50	Share...	General	88jb	Medium	a6ea7f59-7b54-46f8-9e68-5be81172704c	Feature Activation: Activating Feature 'Publishing' (ID:
01/29/2011 14:...	0x2A50	Share...	General	75fb	Medium	a6ea7f59-7b54-46f8-9e68-5be81172704c	Calling 'FeatureActivated' method of SPFeatureReceiv
01/29/2011 14:...	0x2A50	Web ...	Publis...	1ght	High	a6ea7f59-7b54-46f8-9e68-5be81172704c	Publishing Feature activation event handled.
01/29/2011 14:...	0x2A50	Web ...	Publis...	75ot	Unexpec...	a6ea7f59-7b54-46f8-9e68-5be81172704c	Publishing Feature activation failed. Exception: System
01/29/2011 14:...	0x2A50	Share...	Featur...	88jm	High	a6ea7f59-7b54-46f8-9e68-5be81172704c	Feature receiver assembly 'Microsoft.SharePoint.Publi
01/29/2011 14:...	0x2A50	Share...	General	72by	High	a6ea7f59-7b54-46f8-9e68-5be81172704c	Feature Activation: Threw an exception, attempting to
01/29/2011 14:...	0x2A50	Share...	Monito...	b4ly	High	a6ea7f59-7b54-46f8-9e68-5be81172704c	Leaving Monitored Scope (Feature Activation: Activat
01/29/2011 14:...	0x2A50	Share...	General	8l36	High	a6ea7f59-7b54-46f8-9e68-5be81172704c	Failed to activate site-scoped features for template 'BI
01/29/2011 14:...	0x2A50	Share...	Fields	bn3x	High	a6ea7f59-7b54-46f8-9e68-5be81172704c	Failed to activate web features when provisioning site
01/29/2011 14:...	0x2A50	Share...	General	72h9	High	a6ea7f59-7b54-46f8-9e68-5be81172704c	Failed to apply template "BICenterSite#0" to web at U
01/29/2011 14:...	0x2A50	Share...	General	72k2	High	a6ea7f59-7b54-46f8-9e68-5be81172704c	Failed to apply template "BICenterSite#0" to web at U
01/29/2011 14:...	0x2A50	Share...	General	8e1d	High	a6ea7f59-7b54-46f8-9e68-5be81172704c	Deleting the web at http://latide6510-as/BI .
01/29/2011 14:...	0x2A50	Share...	Monito...	b4ly	High	a6ea7f59-7b54-46f8-9e68-5be81172704c	Leaving Monitored Scope (Render WebPart AddGalle
01/29/2011 14:...	0x2A50	Share...	Monito...	b4ly	High	a6ea7f59-7b54-46f8-9e68-5be81172704c	Leaving Monitored Scope (Render WebPart Zone g_
01/29/2011 14:...	0x2A50	Share...	Monito...	b4ly	Medium	a6ea7f59-7b54-46f8-9e68-5be81172704c	Leaving Monitored Scope (Request (POST:http://latid

SharePoint log with a correlation ID

As you can see, this correlation ID is used throughout all log events made during this user's session. This allows great event correlation within a system.

For those who aren't familiar, there is a challenge within development with correlation IDs and specifically it's based on; *when do we use them? Do we use them for everything?* The answer to these questions usually boils down to the type of transaction being made within a system. I will share with you some techniques I've found to be useful, and have brought the most value to Splunk when working on development.

First we need to understand our three most popular actions within an application:

- **Publication**: This is when an application answers a query and publishes data to a user one time. A user clicks a button, the application serves the user it's data for that request, and the transaction is complete.

- **Subscription**: This is a transaction that begins with the click of a button, though the data streams to the user until something stops it. Think of this kind of transaction as a YouTube video that you click on. You click to start the video, and then it just streams to your device. The *stream* is a subscription type of transaction. While the application is serving up this data, it is also often writing to the application logs. This can get noisy as subscriptions can sometimes last hours or even days.

- **Database call**: These are simply calls to a database to either retrieve or insert data to a database. These actions are usually pretty easy to capture. It's what people want to see from this data that becomes a challenge.

Correlation IDs and publication transactions – best practice

It's very simple. Add correlation IDs to all of your publication transactions, and save yourself and your ops team hundreds of hours of troubleshooting.

When writing to a log, if we can log a correlation ID for each publication transaction and insert that data into Splunk, then we can increase the view of what our application is doing tremendously. I will refer to SharePoint again as it is the easiest and most well-known to reference:

Time	Thread	Product	Category	EventID	Level	Correlation	Message
01/29/2011 14:...	0x2A50	Share...	Monito...	b4fy	High	a6ea7f59-7b54-46f8-9e68-5be81172704c	Leaving Monitored Scope (Creating Web Bl). Executio
01/29/2011 14:...	0x2A50	Share...	General	85m6	Medium	a6ea7f59-7b54-46f8-9e68-5be81172704c	Applying web template 'BICenterSite#0' on web url 'htt
01/29/2011 14:...	0x2A50	Share...	General	85m7	Medium	a6ea7f59-7b54-46f8-9e68-5be81172704c	Actual web template to apply to Url http://latide6510-
01/29/2011 14:...	0x2A50	Share...	General	72h7	Medium	a6ea7f59-7b54-46f8-9e68-5be81172704c	Applying template "BICenterSite#0" to web at URL "h
01/29/2011 14:...	0x2A50	Share...	General	83jb	Medium	a6ea7f59-7b54-46f8-9e68-5be81172704c	Feature Activation: Activating Feature 'Publishing' (ID:
01/29/2011 14:...	0x2A50	Share...	General	75fb	Medium	a6ea7f59-7b54-46f8-9e68-5be81172704c	Calling 'FeatureActivated' method of SPFeatureRecen
01/29/2011 14:...	0x2A50	Web ...	Publis...	1ght	High	a6ea7f59-7b54-46f8-9e68-5be81172704c	Publishing Feature activation event handled.
01/29/2011 14:...	0x2A50	Web ...	Publis...	75ot	Unexpec...	a6ea7f59-7b54-46f8-9e68-5be81172704c	Publishing Feature activation failed. Exception: System
01/29/2011 14:...	0x2A50	Share...	Featur...	83jm	High	a6ea7f59-7b54-46f8-9e68-5be81172704c	Feature receiver assembly 'Microsoft.SharePoint.Publi
01/29/2011 14:...	0x2A50	Share...	Monito...	72by	High	a6ea7f59-7b54-46f8-9e68-5be81172704c	Feature Activation: Threw an exception, attempting to
01/29/2011 14:...	0x2A50	Share...	Monito...	b4fy	High	a6ea7f59-7b54-46f8-9e68-5be81172704c	Leaving Monitored Scope (Feature Activation: Activat
01/29/2011 14:...	0x2A50	Share...	General	836	High	a6ea7f59-7b54-46f8-9e68-5be81172704c	Failed to activate site-scoped features for template 'BI
01/29/2011 14:...	0x2A50	Share...	Fields	bn3x	High	a6ea7f59-7b54-46f8-9e68-5be81172704c	Failed to activate web features when provisioning site
01/29/2011 14:...	0x2A50	Share...	General	72h9	High	a6ea7f59-7b54-46f8-9e68-5be81172704c	Failed to apply template "BICenterSite#0" to web at U
01/29/2011 14:...	0x2A50	Share...	General	72k2	High	a6ea7f59-7b54-46f8-9e68-5be81172704c	Failed to apply template "BICenterSite#0" to web at U
01/29/2011 14:...	0x2A50	Share...	General	8e1d	High	a6ea7f59-7b54-46f8-9e68-5be81172704c	Deleting the web at http://latide6510-as/BI .
01/29/2011 14:...	0x2A50	Share...	Monito...	b4fy	High	a6ea7f59-7b54-46f8-9e68-5be81172704c	Leaving Monitored Scope (Render WebPart AddGalle
01/29/2011 14:...	0x2A50	Share...	Monito...	b4fy	High	a6ea7f59-7b54-46f8-9e68-5be81172704c	Leaving Monitored Scope (Render WebPart Zone g_
01/29/2011 14:...	0x2A50	Share...	Monito...	b4fy	Medium	a6ea7f59-7b54-46f8-9e68-5be81172704c	Leaving Monitored Scope (Request (POST http://latid

In the preceding image, all of these events are publications and you can see that it's even written into the log message itself in some events. What we are looking at above is a slice of time a user has been on our system, and their activity.

If we put this data into Splunk, and we extract the correlation ID field correctly, it's as easy as finding a single event with a username and then copying and pasting the correlation ID into our search query to find our user's entire behavior. Above, we are looking at a single instance of SharePoint.

In the real world we may have:

- 200 users
- 10 user-facing machines running an application that is load-balanced
- 30 middleware machines
- 4 databases
- 100+ tables.

Following a single user's activity through that system becomes time consuming, but if we use correlation IDs, mixed with Splunk, we will find ourselves saving days of time when looking for problems. We can also proactively alert on our system if we extract the knowledge in Splunk properly.

Developers actually love correlation IDs more than operations, because inserting their application data into Splunk and allowing them a single place to search the logs of their applications where all they have to do is find the correlation ID to look for a user's activity saves lots of time in QA.

Correlation IDs and subscription transactions – best practices

The most common question for subscription transactions and correlation IDs is; How can we minimize the wasted space in the log that arises from subscription events, seeing as they are part of the same transaction and don't need to be written to every event within each subscription?

For subscription type events within a log, they are commonly very noisy and not needed until something breaks.

The compromise for writing correlation IDs to let Splunk continue to monitor user activity is to write a correlation ID in the event only at subscription start and subscription end.

If you want further detail on your subscriptions, and you want Splunk to be able to quickly retrieve these events, the developers I've known have used subscription IDs, which are printed to the log with every action within a subscription transaction. These are also usually GUIDs, but they target only a user's subscription within your system.

This often ends up being seen most in Splunk license utilization. However, if we plan accordingly, we can subvert this issue in the real world.

Correlation IDs and database calls – best practices

In this type of transaction we can write a correlation ID each time a transaction occurs, the same way we would do as a publication. As best practice, write this ID to the log event in the same manner one would on a publication transaction.

The larger the system, the more chaos we as Splunk experts must try to bring some order to. In many cases, companies have a specific use case for something like Splunk, though they often expect that Splunk is a turnkey solution.

Unstructured data

The following screenshot is an example of what unstructured data looks like:

```
weblogic.application.utils.StateMachineDriver.nextState(StateMachineDriver.java:26)
>
####<Dec 29, 2006 2:14:24 PM IST> <Notice> <Log Management> <svaidyan02> <xbusServer>
<[ACTIVE] ExecuteThread: '0' for queue: 'weblogic.kernel.Default (self-tuning)'> <<WLS
Kernel>> <> <> <1167381864275> <BEA-170027> <The server initialized the domain log
broadcaster successfully. Log messages will now be broadcasted to the domain log.>
####<Dec 29, 2006 2:14:24 PM IST> <Notice> <WebLogicServer> <svaidyan02> <xbusServer> <Main
Thread> <<WLS Kernel>> <> <> <1167381864976> <BEA-000365> <Server state changed to ADMIN>
####<Dec 29, 2006 2:14:24 PM IST> <Notice> <WebLogicServer> <svaidyan02> <xbusServer> <Main
Thread> <<WLS Kernel>> <> <> <1167381864996> <BEA-000365> <Server state changed to RESUMING>
####<Dec 29, 2006 2:14:28 PM IST> <Notice> <Security> <svaidyan02> <xbusServer> <[STANDBY]
ExecuteThread: '5' for queue: 'weblogic.kernel.Default (self-tuning)'> <<WLS Kernel>> <> <>
<1167381868541> <BEA-090171> <Loading the identity certificate and private key stored under
the alias DemoIdentity from the jks keystore file
C:\bea2613a\WEBLOG~1\server\lib\DemoIdentity.jks.>
####<Dec 29, 2006 2:14:29 PM IST> <Notice> <Security> <svaidyan02> <xbusServer> <[STANDBY]
ExecuteThread: '5' for queue: 'weblogic.kernel.Default (self-tuning)'> <<WLS Kernel>> <> <>
<1167381869643> <BEA-090169> <Loading trusted certificates from the jks keystore file
C:\bea2613a\WEBLOG~1\server\lib\DemoTrust.jks.>
####<Dec 29, 2006 2:14:29 PM IST> <Notice> <Security> <svaidyan02> <xbusServer> <[STANDBY]
ExecuteThread: '5' for queue: 'weblogic.kernel.Default (self-tuning)'> <<WLS Kernel>> <> <>
<1167381869713> <BEA-090169> <Loading trusted certificates from the jks keystore file
C:\bea2613a\JROCKI~1\jre\lib\security\cacerts.>
####<Dec 29, 2006 2:15:32 PM IST> <Warning> <Server> <svaidyan02> <xbusServer>
<DynamicSSLListenThread[DefaultSecure[1]]> <<WLS Kernel>> <> <> <1167381932743> <BEA-002611>
<Hostname "svaidyan02.apac.bea.com", maps to multiple IP addresses: 192.168.1.5,
172.22.56.120>
####<Dec 29, 2006 2:15:32 PM IST> <Notice> <Server> <svaidyan02> <xbusServer> <[STANDBY]
ExecuteThread: '5' for queue: 'weblogic.kernel.Default (self-tuning)'> <<WLS Kernel>> <> <>
<1167381932753> <BEA-002613> <Channel "Default[2]" is now listening on 127.0.0.1:7021 for
```

These kinds of logs are much more complicated to bring value to, as all of the knowledge must be manually extracted by a Splunk engineer or admin. Splunk will look at your data and attempt to extract things that it believes is fields. However, this often ends up being nothing of what you or your users are wanting to use to add value to their dashboards.

That being the case, this is where one would need to speak to the developer/vendor of that specific software, and start asking some pointed questions.

In these kinds of logs, before we can start adding the proper value, there are some foundational elements that need to be correct. I'm only going to focus on the first, as we will get to the other 2 later in this book.

- Time stamping
- Event breaking
- Event definitions
- Field definitions (field mapping)

Event breaking – best practice

With structured data, Splunk will usually see the events and not automatically break them as they are nice and orderly.

With unstructured data, in order to make sure we are getting the data in appropriately, the events need to be in some sort of organized chaos, and this usually begins with breaking an event at the appropriate line/character in the log. There's lots of ways to break an event in Splunk (see `http://docs.splunk.com/Documentation/Splunk/6.4.1/Admin/Propsconf` and search for `break`), but using the preceding data, we are going to be looking at the timestamp to reference where we should break these events, as using the first field, which is most often the timestamp, is the most effective way to break an event.

There are a few questions to ask yourself when breaking events, though one of the more important questions is; *are these events all in one line, or are there multiple lines in each event?* If you don't know the answer to this question, ask the SME (dev/vendor). Things can get messy once data is in, so save yourself a bit of time by asking this question before inputting data.

In the following example, we can see the timestamp is the event delimiter and that there can be multiple lines in an event. This means that we need to break events pre-indexing:

```
01/08/2016 07:28:54.100 - 1 home 1 New Home Avenue2 dentist
01/08/2016 07:28:54.430 - 1 DDS Avenue3 la 3 LA shack3 restaurant 3
Hole in the wall 7 dev house
Kelld 7 NO fowlerville MPPN  November 14
November 22 2015 - Inst 8876.33_v2 filled for Caption at fox 2
01/08/2016 07:29:54.010 - 7 Hacker way dist 55v12bb CANCELLED X11253581 Order From 223
APPT 8874698225
```

In order to do that, we need to adjust our `props.conf` on our indexer. Doing so will appropriately delineate log events as noted in the following image:

```
01/08/2016 07:28:54.100 - 1 home 1 New Home Avenue2 dentist
01/08/2016 07:28:54.430 - 1 DDS Avenue3 la 3 LA shack3 restaurant 3
Hole in the wall 7 dev house
Kelld 7 NO fowlerville MPPN  November 14
November 22 2015 - Inst 8876.33_v2 filled for Caption at fox 2
01/08/2016 07:29:54.010 - 7 Hacker way dist 55v12bb CANCELLED X11253581 Order From 223
APPT 8874698225
```

Adding line breaking to the indexing tier in this way is a method for pre-index event breaking and data cannot be removed without cleaning an index.

In this example, we have five indexers in a cluster pool, so using the UI on each of those indexers is not recommended. "Why?" you ask. In short, once you cluster your indexers, most of the files that would end up in `$SPLUNK_HOME/etc/` having become shared, and they must be pushed as a bundle by the cluster master. It is also not recommended by Splunk support. Try it if you like, but be prepared for some long nights.

Currently Splunk is set up to do this quite easily from an individual file via the UI, though when dealing with a larger infrastructure and multiple indexers, the UI feature often isn't the best way to admin. As a tip, if you're an admin and you don't have a personal instance of Splunk installed on your workstation for just this purpose, install one. Testing the features you will implement is often the best practice of any system.

Best practices

Why should you install an instance of Splunk on your personal workstation you ask? Because if you bump into an issue where you need to index a dataset that you can't use the UI for, you can get a subset of the data in a file and attempt to ingest it into your personal instance while leveraging the UI and all its neat features. Then just copy all of the relevant settings to your indexers/cluster master. This is how you can do that:

1. Get a subset of the data, the SME can copy and paste it in an e-mail, or send it attached or by any other way, just get the subset so you can try to input it. Save it to the machine that is running your personal Splunk instance.

2. Login to your personal Splunk instance and attempt to input the data. In Splunk, go to **Settings** | **Data Inputs** | **Files & Directories** | **New** and select your file which should bring you to a screen that looks like this:

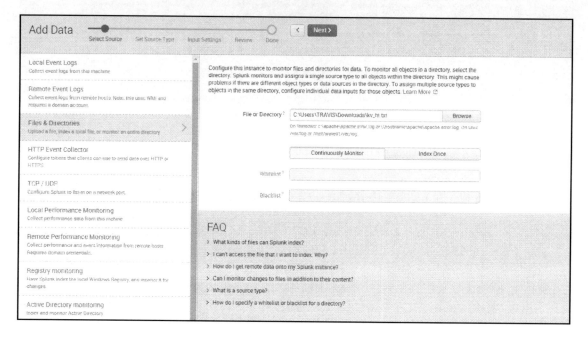

3. Attempt to break your events using the UI.

Now we are going to let Splunk do most of the configuring here. We have three ways to do this:

1. **Auto:** Let Splunk do the figuring.
2. **Every Line**: this is self-explanatory.
3. **Regex…**: use a REGEX to tell Splunk where each line starts.

For this example, I'm going to say we spoke to the developer and they actually did say that the timestamp was the event divider. It looks like Auto will do just fine, as Splunk naturally breaks events at timestamps:

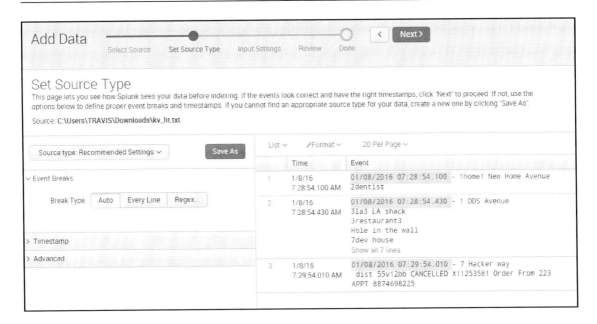

Going down the rest of the option, we can leave the timestamp extraction to **Auto** as well, because it's easily readable in the log.

The **Advanced** tab is for adding settings manually, but for this example and the information we have, we won't need to worry about it.

When we click the **Next** button we can set our source type, and we want to pay attention to the **App** portion of this, for the future. That is where the configuration we are building will be saved:

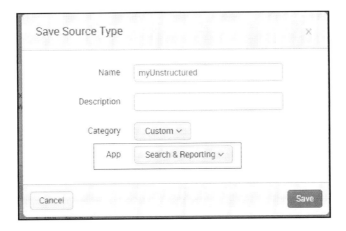

Click **Save** and set all of the other values on the next couple of windows as well if you like. As this is your personal Splunk instance, it's not terribly important because you, the Splunk admin, are the only person who will see it.

When you're finished make sure your data looks like you expect it to in a search:

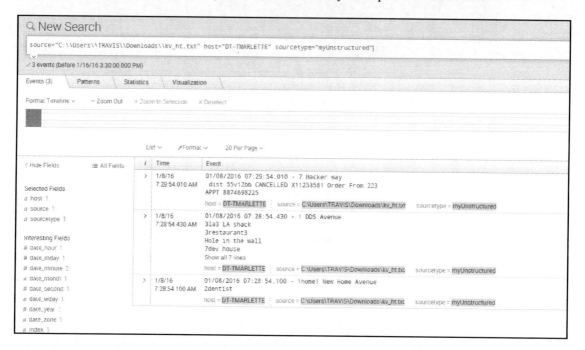

And if you're happy with it (and let's say we are) we can then look at moving this configuration to our cluster.

Remember when I mentioned we should pay attention to the **App**? That's where the configuration that we want was written. At this point, it's pretty much just copying and pasting.

Configuration transfer – best practice

All of that was only to get Splunk to auto-generate the configuration that you need to break your data, so the next step is just transferring that configuration to a cluster.

You'll need two files for this. The `props.conf` that we just edited on your personal instance, and the `props.conf` on your cluster master. (For those of you unfamiliar, `$SPLUNK_HOME/etc/master_apps/` on your cluster master)

This was the config that Splunk just wrote in my personal instance of Splunk:

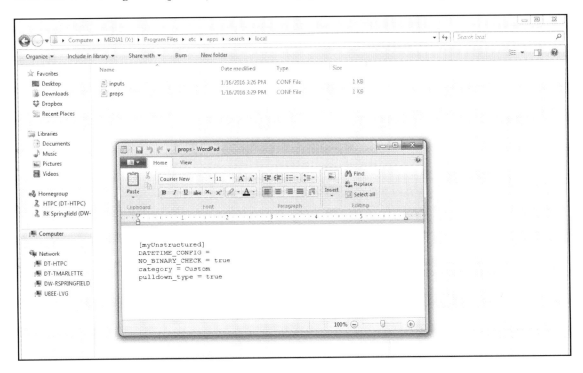

Follow these steps to transfer the configuration:

1. Go the destination app's `props.conf`, copy the configuration and paste it to your cluster masters `props.conf`, then distribute the configuration to its peers (`$SPLUNK_HOME/etc/master_apps/props.conf`). In the case of our example:

   ```
   Copy source file =
   $SPLUNK_HOME/etc/apps/search/local/props.conf
   Copy dest file = $SPLUNK_HOME/etc/master_apps/props.conf
   ```

2. Change the stanza to your source type in the cluster:
   - When we pasted our configuration into our cluster master, it looked like this:

   ```
   [myUnstructured]
   DATETIME_CONFIG =
   NO_BINARY_CHECK = true
   category = Custom
   pulldown_type = true
   ```

   - Yet there is no myUnstructured source type in the production cluster. In order to make these changes take effect on your production source type, just adjust the name of the stanza. In our example we will say that the log snippet we received was from a web frontend, which is the name of our source type.
   - The change would look like this:

   ```
   [web_frontend]
   DATETIME_CONFIG =
   NO_BINARY_CHECK = true
   category = Custom
   pulldown_type = true
   ```

3. Push the cluster bundle via the UI on the cluster master:

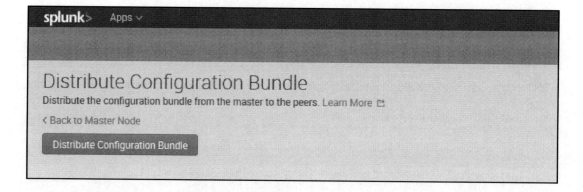

4. Make sure your data looks the way you want it to:

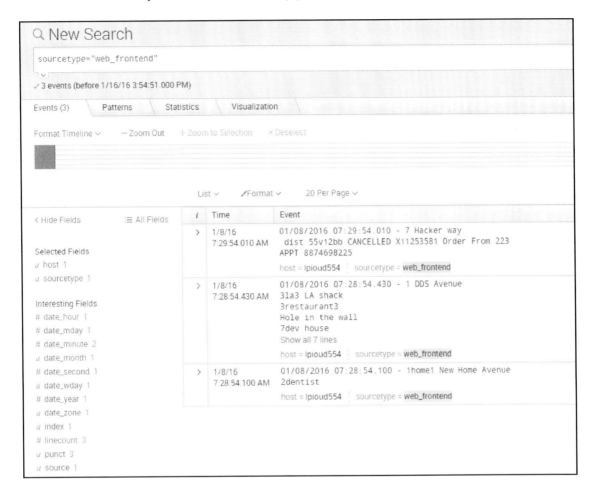

Once we have it coming into our index in some sort of reasonable chaos, we can begin extracting knowledge from events.

Summary

In this chapter we discussed where the lion's share of application data comes from and how that data gets into Splunk and how Splunk reacts to it. We mentioned good ways and things to keep in mind when developing applications, or scripts, and also how to adjust Splunk to handle some non-standardized logging. Splunk is as turnkey as the data you put into it. Meaning, if you have a 20-year-old application that logs unstructured data in debug mode only, your Splunk instance will not be turnkey. With a system like Splunk, we can quote some data science experts in saying *garbage in, garbage out*.

While I say that, I will add an addendum by saying that Splunk, mixed with a Splunk expert and the right development resources, can also make the data I just mentioned extremely valuable. It will likely not happen as fast as they make it out to be at a presentation, and it will take more resources than you may have thought. However, at the end of your Splunk journey, you will be happy. This chapter was to help you understand the importance of logs formatting and how logs are written. We often don't think about our logs proactively and I encourage you to do so.

Now that we have this understanding about logging and the types of data that applications generally write, we can move on to understanding what kinds of data inputs Splunk uses in order to get data in.

Determining which data input suits your use case is often the first part of getting data into Splunk, and with a wide variety of ways to do this, Splunk enables us to use the methods that they have developed, as well as allowing room for us to develop our own if necessary.

2
Data Inputs

In Splunk there are many ways to get data into the indexers, which make for the ability to be very creative in doing so. Between the apps that are provided on Splunk base and the other methods that can be developed by an individual, it paves the way to be very dynamic in getting data in to get value out of your data.

In this chapter I'm going to assume that you have your Forwarders installed.

Let's start with most of the agents and applications to get data into Splunk.

Agents

These are the thin and thick clients from Splunk that can be used to forward data to Splunk.

Splunk Universal Forwarder

Splunk Universal Forwarder is a light agent that is installed on a device that enables you with quite a bit of functionality to get data into a Splunk index. The name is pretty self-explanatory, as this agent is designed to simply forward data to a Splunk index. This is often the most common method to get data into Splunk.

Splunk Heavy Forwarder

This is a heavy agent. It is basically a full version of Splunk that is installed on a device in order to perform the same data-forwarding functionality as the Universal Forwarder, with the added benefit of being able to perform some more complex functions.

It is often used as a centralized point for data gathering of multiple systems, as well as a data router to collect, route, and scrub data appropriately before it hits an indexer. These are usually standalone machines within your Splunk infrastructure.

Search Head Forwarder

If you have limited ability to create an infrastructure, or you have security limitations within your environment, you can also use your Search Head as a Heavy Forwarder as it has all of the essential functionality of a Heavy Forwarder. This can be resource intensive depending on how many data inputs you are pumping into your indexers, so mind the resource utilization if you use this method.

Data inputs

Knowing all of the applications and methods we can use to get data into Splunk, let's talk about the types of data inputs from data sources, and how they get to the indexer. There are six general types of data inputs in Splunk:

- API inputs
- Database inputs
- Monitoring inputs
- Scripted inputs
- Modular inputs
- Windows inputs

API inputs

There are two ways to get REST API data into Splunk:

- Download the REST API modular input, and install it into your Heavy Forwarder
- Write a REST API poller using **cURL** or some other method to query the API, and scrub the output for the data you need

If at all possible, use the REST API modular input from Splunk, as it is very easy to set up and use. Just figure out your URL, and set up the API input and it's interval that you want it to be polled at.

Q: When would you ever use a custom API input if Splunk already has a REST API input available?

A: When one doesn't already exist, and it's the only way to get data from your system.

An example of this is MapR's newest version called **YARN**. MR1 doesn't have an API that is very useful for gathering metrics, but YARN on the other hand has a device called **History Server** which retains all job metrics for any running, or a job that already been run. However, there is no prebuilt API for this, so you would need to develop one.

Methods of writing an API input are left up to the developer; however, I know that when using Splunk, Python is a very common and effective language to get the job done.

Database inputs

These are usually the most popular of the input sets, simply because writing your own DB connector can be resource intensive, and publishing your database information in a system such as Splunk usually adds a lot of value to your dashboards. For these, use DB Connect; it is plain and simple, because the heavy lifting has already been done for you by the developers at Splunk. DB Connect requires either a Heavy Forwarder or a Search Head and there are a couple of ways to get data from your database. I won't discuss database inputs here, as they require an installation of DB Connect which can be a challenge in and of itself. I will simply refer you to the link to the Splunk website for how to create DB inputs leveraging DB Connect 2.0:

```
http://docs.splunk.com/Documentation/DBX/latest/DeployDBX/Createandmanagedataba
seinputs
```

The different type of database inputs that DB Connect can leverage are as follows:

- **Automated input**: These are simply scheduled to run on a time interval, and ingest the whole table that you target.
- **Rising column**: These inputs can simply watch your unique key in your database and add only the newest rows of data.
- **Dynamic queries** (Search Head Forwarder only): These are queries (often SQL) that are written into your search queries. These DB queries can be modified by a DB admin to show only the data that a user would want to see instead of the entire table.
- **DB lookups** (Search Head Forwarder only): These are queries that you can set within DB Connect to lookup things such as employee numbers, or product IDs from a database. You can either use them to lookup data on the fly, or you can write the results to a lookup file or your key-value store.

DB Connect formats any of this data into happy `key=value` pairs for you to easily parse and search through. DB Connect has compatibility with SQL, MySQL, DB2, Oracle, MongoDB, and more. Feel free to check your DB compatibility at `http://www.splunk.com /.`

DB Connect can be a bear to install depending on your security and your system. When installing this app, follow the walk-through at `http://www. splunk.com/`. I'm not a fan of instructions, especially when they are as long as they are with DB Connect, but in this case I recommend following them closely to keep your sanity.

Monitoring inputs

This is literally just monitoring a file, be it text based, XML, or JSON. The more structured the file, and the more well behaved the logging, the easier it is to get into Splunk. Generally, Splunk likes flat files, however there are still frustrations that come along with this depending on what you monitor.

Scripted inputs

A scripted input is literally a script that can be deployed by the deployment server, run and collect data. The most popular language to use for creating these scripts is bash, Python, PowerShell, or Perl.

When using Perl or Python, make sure that whatever libraries you are using when creating a script are within the standard Splunk Forwarder installation, or on your machine. The JSON package (for instance) is not included on some systems (maybe for security, or just a choice by the admin) so if you need to use it to print your output to a nice friendly JSON format, be sure to include it in your deployment server application and reference it accordingly in your script.

If you have ever deployed the Splunk Linux add-on, you have deployed a series of bash scripts on every one of your Linux systems, and they run to collect data from different standard system command outputs.

The beauty of the scripted input is that the script you create only has to echo or print the output, and the Forwarder takes care of the rest.

I'll use a real-world example for this, as I know sometimes server inventory can be problematic depending on the company.

Custom or not

These are inputs that are written in a scripting language. Often in Linux, these are written in bash, but if we need to talk to Windows we can use more versatile languages such as Python, Perl, or PowerShell as well. Each Forwarder comes with a set of libraries for languages such as Python, or Perl, but for languages such as PowerShell or bash, the Forwarder will use the libraries that are installed on the system itself. With PowerShell, it's advised to install the PowerShell add-on from Splunk in order to leverage that language appropriately. When you do it's simply a stanza within your `inputs.conf` you can set at an interval of time to collect the data.

> In this example, we have 2400+ Forwarders (Linux), 15 indexers (clustered), and 5 Search Heads (4 pooled, 1 solo).

The problems are:

- With so many machines, virtual machines, and physical machines being spun up and retired every day, how do we keep track of that entire inventory?
- Can we dynamically track the Hadoop nodes cluster participation?

The solution is:

To use Splunk to deploy a scripted input that runs twice a week to gather metrics, automate a report, and e-mail it to the data center teams.

When there are so many machines, a deployment server is absolutely necessary, and fortunately it's a single source to deploy to a major deployment. If you can, write a single script to work on one Linux machine then just deploy it to the rest using Splunk.

In this instance, most of the 1400 nodes were part of multiple Hadoop clusters (I believe we had 24 or so), and as machines spun up, went down, or got replaced, the machines would be named freshly according to their location within the data center. Meaning that not only can the machines change, but so can their IPs.

The method used to track them was that a person would have to sit down every week and go through the tickets to determine which machines were live, and which had been moved and retired. With so many machines, I can only imagine what that person's life must have been like, considering, from a business perspective, that this was the person's only job. A dedicated resource (regardless of the cost) was needed in order to track such inventory on a scale like that.

In our environment, we were fortunate to have the Splunk Universal Forwarder on every node, as Splunk was purchased in order to help manage the big data infrastructure.

This is part of the script that was written:

```
SERVERNAME=`uname -n | awk -F "." '{ print $1 }'`
CLUSTER=`cat /etc/profile | grep PS1 | grep -oP '\[\(\K[^\)]+'`
PROC_COUNT=`cat /proc/cpuinfo | grep processor | wc -l`
SOCKETS=`cat /proc/cpuinfo | egrep 'physical id' | sort -u | wc -l`
CORES=`cat /proc/cpuinfo | egrep 'cpu cores' | sort -u | awk '{ print $4
}'`
UPTIME=` uptime |awk '{print $3" "$4" "$5}'`
MEMKB=`cat /proc/meminfo | grep MemTotal | awk '{ print $2 }'`
MEMORY=`expr $MEMKB / 1048576`
OS=`uname -s`
OSVERSION=`cat /etc/redhat-release   |awk '{print $0}'`
KERNAL=`uname -a | awk '{ print \$3 }'`
OS_MANUFACTURER=`cat /etc/redhat-release   |awk '{print $1" "$2}'`

SERIAL_NUMBER=`dmidecode -s system-serial-number`
SERVER_TYPE=''
if [[ $SERIAL_NUMBER =~ ^VMwa ]]; then
                SERVER_TYPE="Virtual"
                    else SERVER_TYPE="Physical"
fi
SPEED=`cat /proc/cpuinfo | grep MHz | tail -1 | awk '{ print $4 }'`
CPU_TYPE=`cat /proc/cpuinfo | grep '^model name' | awk -F: '{ print $2 }' |
tail -1`
DISKS=`lsblk -ibo KNAME,TYPE,SIZE,MODEL | grep disk | wc -l`
MODEL=`lshal | grep -i 'system.hardware.product' | awk -F' '{ print $2 }'`
MANUFACTURER=`lshal | grep -i 'system.hardware.vendor' | awk -F' '{ print
$2 }'`
#NIC=`/sbin/ifconfig -a |grep -i -B 3 "UP" |grep -i "HWaddr"| awk '{print
$1}'`
#MAC_ADDR=`/sbin/ifconfig -a |grep -i -B 3 "UP" |grep -i "HWaddr"| awk
'{print $5}'`
INSTALL_DATE=`ls -l /root/install.log |awk '{print $6, $7, $8}'`
#IP_ADDR=`hostname -i |awk '{print \$0}'`
TIMESTAMP=`date +"%F %T %Z"`

echo -n "$TIMESTAMP | cluster=$CLUSTER | serverName=$SERVERNAME |
serverType=$SERVER_TYPE | procCount=$PROC_COUNT | sockets=$SOCKETS |
cores=$CORES | uptime="$UPTIME" | memory=$MEMORY | os=$OS |
osVersion="$OSVERSION" | kernalVersion=$KERNAL |
osManufacturer="$OS_MANUFACTURER" | SN="$SERIAL_NUMBER" | cpuSpeed=$SPEED |
cpuType="$CPU_TYPE" | diskCount=$DISKS | model="$MODEL" |
manufacurer="$MANUFACTURER" | installDate="$INSTALL_DATE" | "
```

If you put this script in a file and execute the script, the output comes in a nice pleasant `key=value` format like this:

```
serverName=myMachineName | cluster=hadoopCluster1 | timeStamp="2016-02-06
20:28:15 MST" | serverType=Physical | procCount=32 | sockets=2 | cores=8 |
uptime="200 days, 4:17," | memory=125 | os=Linux | osVersion="Red Hat
Enterprise Linux Server release 6.4 (Santiago)" |
kernalVersion=2.6.32-358.el6.x86_64 | osManufacturer="Red Hat" |
SN="FCH181BB3XY" | cpuSpeed=2599.929 | cpuType=" Intel(R) Xeon(R) CPU
E5-2650 v2 @ 2.60GHz" | diskCount=2 | model="UCSC-C240-M3S" |
manufacurer="Cisco Systems Inc" | installDate="May 8 2014
```

Which Splunk loves:

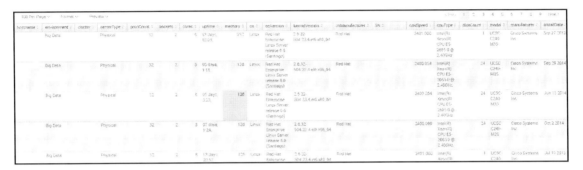

After the script was created, the deployment was made to all machines using the deployment server.

 I figured it's a given, but I will mention this just in case. Make sure the Universal Forwarder is running as an account that has access to run all of your desired commands. Without proper permissions, no script will work.

Modular inputs

These inputs are usually installed on a Heavy Forwarder, and collect data from multiple sources. Let's use the simple example of **SNMP(Simple Network Management Protocol)** polling, as well as an API modular input. Both of these packages can be installed on the same Heavy Forwarder, and while SNMP is polling your network devices, maybe the API modular input is polling a REST API of your Resource Manager device to draw information about Hadoop jobs for your **YARN (Yet Another Resource Negotiator)** system. For these you can use the UI of the Heavy Forwarder to set them up.

These inputs can be developed by you, or they also often come packaged within many apps from Splunk. A modular input is usually best recognized for being able to use the UI in order to configure it. Some apps that leverage modular inputs are the EMC app for Xtreme IO, the SNMP modular input, and the REST API input.

Often these inputs leverage backend code or scripting that reach out to the target system and speak to the systems API, pull back a bunch of data, and format the data output into a meaningful format.

Many companies have partnered with Splunk in order to create an app that leverages a modular input. The EMC Xtreme app on Splunk is a great example of that, as is the Service Now app. These apps were developed (and are supported) by both Splunk and the company, so if you get stuck in deploying an app like this, first call Splunk, and (if needed) they can reach out to the company.

Modular inputs can be difficult to develop, however they are quite easy to use, which makes the effort in pre-deployment worth it. Often, Splunk admins simply don't have the time to make these, which is when Splunkbase is a wonderful thing.

We will just use an app from Splunkbase to show what a modular input looks like, and how to recognize one.

The EMX XtremIO add-on is a modular input. This is best installed on either a Search Head Forwarder or a Heavy Forwarder for the purpose of saving you time getting the data from the system to a Splunk index:

EMC XtremIO Add-on for Splunk Enterprise

This technology add-on collects data from EMC XtremIO cluster to be used by the EMC XtremIO App for Splunk Enterprise.

Content: Add-on | **Compatibility:** 6.2 | **Platform:** Platform Independent | **Categories:** IT Operations Management | **Author:** Crest Data Systems | **Downloads:** 85 | **Released:** Jul 31, 2015 | **Updated:** Jul 31, 2015

This is necessary in order to get data into Splunk from your Xtreme IO appliance, and is part of the installation bundle for the Xtreme IO app.

 Often apps come with multiple pieces, as the app itself is usually just a set of dashboards and knowledge objects in order to visualize the data from the system. That data is usually gathered by a Heavy Forwarder, or an instance of DB Connect, and is also usually quite a bit more complicated to install than the app itself. To reiterate, often apps on Splunkbase are just visualizations, and without the rest of the package that gathers the data, they will remain blank.

If you're getting into things like this, it's always best to set up a Heavy Forwarder, and install the app there. That way you can offload the data gathering tasks from your Search Head and let the Heavy Forwarder do the work:

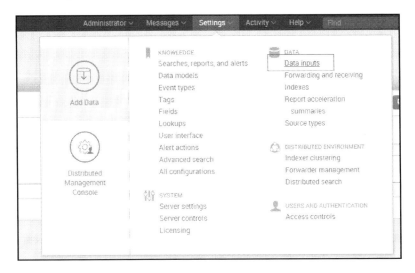

When you install this kind of add-on to your Heavy Forwarder, you generally won't get a standard app icon within the app selection menu. Since this is a data input, it will be a new selection under the **Data inputs** menu:

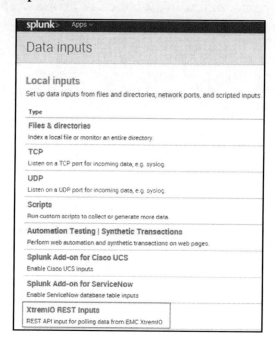

Now you can see that this modular input leverages a REST API for gathering its data. Many times this is the case, but not always. If we click on this when it is unconfigured you will see that it's blank, and that there is no way to configure it. With Splunk you can rest assured that there is always at least one way to do this; however, we hope for two:

- The easy way:
    - This is when someone has been kind enough to develop a UI configuration setup tool within their modular input to assist in the setup process.
- The hard way:
    - This is when we have to go to the backend and manually configure stanzas and settings that are specific to the app. That means time spent in research trying to discover the settings that are necessary for your system.

In our example, we will use the easy way, because someone was nice enough to develop an interface for this.

It's not always intuitive to find the configuration setup utility for a Splunk app, as is in this case; however, let's not cry over spilled milk.

To find this modular inputs setup utility, just go to your standard app menu, and select **Manage Apps**:

When you do find your app, you should notice a **Set up** button under the **Actions** column:

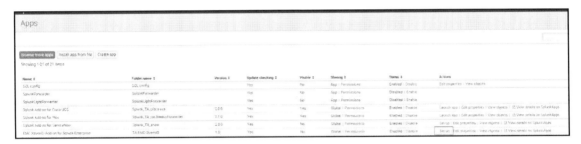

In this case, it's as easy as entering the IP (or DNS address) of your appliance, a **Username** with appropriate permissions and that user's **Password**, and clicking **Save**:

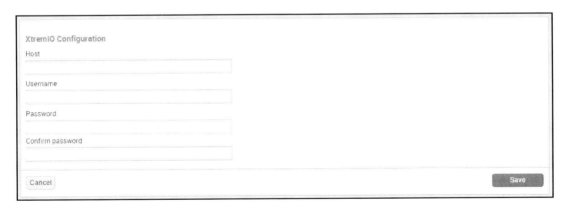

Confirm that your new data inputs were created by going back to the **Data inputs** menu, and clicking your modular input:

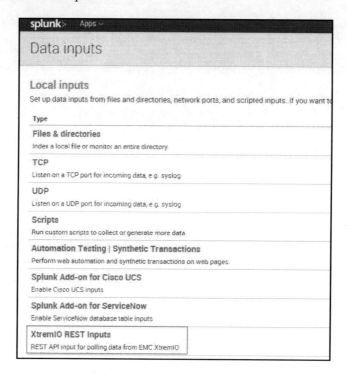

And you should see this:

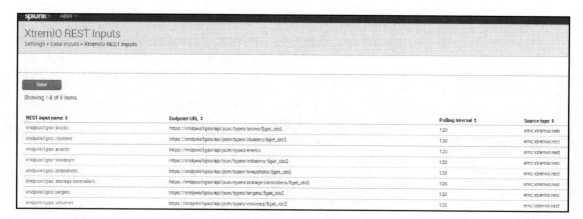

After that, just set your intervals if you like, and enable them all, and you should be able to see some data. If not, do a search on `index=_internal` for your app, and troubleshoot accordingly.

Now that we know some good use cases for our inputs, we can start to organize the chaos that we have been dumping into Splunk.

Windows inputs

These are pretty much fully packaged within Splunk, and the apps developed by Splunk. Windows can be a tricky animal, so we appreciate the people at Splunk making this as easy as they have.

Each input simply has a different stanza within the Forwarders `inputs.conf`. That stanza leverages the Windows API in order to get its data from Windows. These are mainly covered in the Windows add-on for Splunk. Here are examples of a couple of stanzas from a default `inputs.conf` file in that app. If you choose to use the default stanzas, pay special attention to the `checkpointInterval` setting. By default, it is set to 30 seconds. If that is more frequent than you need this can result in a higher than necessary license impact:

```
[WinEventLog://Application]
disabled = 0
start_from = oldest
current_only = 0
checkpointInterval = 10
index = yourIndexName
renderXml=false

[perfmon://CPU]
counters = % Processor Time; % User Time; % Privileged Time;
Interrupts/sec; % DPC Time; % Interrupt Time; DPCs Queued/sec; DPC Rate; %
Idle Time; % C1 Time; % C2 Time; % C3 Time; C1 Transitions/sec; C2
Transitions/sec; C3 Transitions/sec
disabled = 0
instances = *
interval = 30
object = Processor
useEnglishOnly=true
index = yourIndexName
```

The `index` name can be changed in this app. However, all of the searches within the windows app expect to find data in the indexes specified in the default configuration. If you customize the indexes, you'll have to go through the app to find where you broke it. Often the apps are made by leveraging a general search macro, or an event type, so be sure to check the app's `macros.conf` and `eventtypes.conf` for the old index name and change it before you start going through every dashboard and search query.

Windows event logs / Perfmon

Windows is a tricky system to get system data from, though the people at Splunk have eased this process considerably. Splunk has been kind enough to write into their software a way to decode Windows event logs using an API. This helps greatly in the extraction of Windows event logs, as all Windows logs are written in binary and are quite unintelligible to look at in their raw state.

If you're using Windows, you'll need to use a Splunk Universal Forwarder or Heavy Forwarder to pull data in this fashion, although I assure you it's far easier than crafting your own PowerShell scripts or WMI queries to get the data.

Deployment server

Now that we know what types of data inputs there are, let's say that you have 500 Forwarders and they are different parts of unique systems. How do you manage all of that?

I've got three words for you: **Splunk deployment server**.

If you're not familiar with Splunk deployment server, I highly recommend you become familiar. With a large deployment of Splunk it's surely the easiest way to manage all of your data inputs for your various systems:

- **Basics**: As a general rule of thumb, in Splunk best practices, in Splunk architecture, there should be at least one deployment server. That deployment server would sit behind a load balancing device (let's use *F5*) and have its own DNS address.
- **Reason**: Because if anything ever happens to your DS, and it has a catastrophic failure, what happens when you need to spin up a new one and you can't have the same IP address? Assuming that you don't have a system such as Puppet, Chef, or StackIQ to use to manage your infrastructure, that means you've got a long couple of days of logging on to all 500 machines to change a single setting in

`deploymentclient.conf` on every host. It's much easier to put this behind a DNS address, and then change your DNS record when your machine gets a new IP address.

- **Machine Specs**: For a DS, it generally doesn't have to be very bulky. If you use these metrics it will give you a good idea of how to size your dedicated deployment server:
  - *8 cores + 8GB RAM = ~3000 – 4000 deployment clients* (default settings)

A deployment server usually can handle quite a few clients, as the only thing it usually does is get a heartbeat every 5 minutes from each client, and then once in a while it will upload new configurations to systems when you reload your server classes.

There are three basic parts to the Splunk deployment server:

- **Serverclass.conf**: In the `/etc/system/local/` folder of the deployment server, when you create a file called `serverclass.conf`, you've just installed a deployment server. That's pretty much it. The rest is all the configuration of the deployment server.
- **Deploymentclient.conf**: This is in the `/etc/system/local/` folder of each Forwarder that you want to be managed by the deployment server. Once installed, restart Splunk, and look for the reported Forwarders.
- **App Repository**: This is usually the `/etc/deployment-apps/` folder on the deployment server itself. This is where you will keep the configurations and files that you want to push to your deployment.

Now, before we get into deploying apps, let me preface this by saying that if you use the deployment server to manage your core Splunk infrastructure, be aware of a couple of things:

- The deployment server is not supported in any clustered configuration of Splunk. This is directly from Splunk. The reason for this is because in order to do this successfully you need a very thorough understanding of folder hierarchy in Splunk. Each cluster of Splunk core has its own **master node** if you will, that trumps anything that the deployment server will deploy.
- Using the deployment server to install things such as DB Connect is also not supported by Splunk. There are far too many complexities in apps such as DB Connect that will require you to manage the machine manually.

In best practices, limiting your configuration within the deployment server to monitor, scripted, or Windows type inputs is going to make your life easier. Once you have a firm grasp of these, and you've installed things such as DB Connect and Custom API inputs, you'll better understand why these are not easily managed with the deployment server.

 When installing a Forwarder, it is often best to leave it completely configured except the `deploymentclient.conf`, and then just let the deployment server configure this once a Forwarder contacts it.

Now I'm going to give an example of how to manage an OS metric from a scripted input, and deploy it to your 500 Linux machines. This one input can be replicated as many times as you like for your scripts.

 In this example, I have 1 Search Head, 1 indexer, and 500 Linux Universal Forwarders.

First, let's make sure we can connect to our deployment server from our Forwarder.

To do this we run a simple telnet test to the IP and port of the deployment server:

```
telnet mydeploymentserver.com 8089
```

If telnet is shut off in your environment for security but `SSH` is still available, use this:

```
ssh -v -p 8089 mydeploymentserver.com
```

If we can't connect, then we have a firewall problem somewhere, so track that down and open your firewall. In our example, our firewall is already open.

In the `/etc/system/local/` folder of my deployment server is the `serverclass.conf` file, with these settings at the top:

```
[global]
disabled = false
repositoryLocation = $SPLUNK_HOME/etc/deployment-apps
restartSplunkd = true
whitelist.0 = *
```

So now we've told Splunk that the deployment server is active, and given it a very general step to take if a Forwarder contacts it.

Now let's go to our Forwarders.

 In this I will assume manual installations of your Forwarders are necessary; however, in Linux you can write a script to perform this action. For an example of such, just follow this link: `https://answers.splunk.com/answers/34896/simple-installation-script-for-universal-forwarder.html`.

When we install our Forwarders, we just run a `tar -xf` command in the `/opt/ folder` (or whichever folder you prefer), accept the license, and then configure our file.

On the Forwarder, we need to navigate to `/etc/system/local/` and look for `deploymentclient.conf`. If the file does not exist, create it using a text editor.

In `/etc/system/local/deploymentclient.conf` on the Forwarder, we add these settings:

```
[deployment-client]
disabled = false
clientName = MyLinuxEnvironment

[target-broker:deploymentServer]
targetUri = mydeploymentserver.com:8089
```

The `targetUri` can be a hostname, or an IP address as well, and `8089` is the default management port for Splunk. If you need to change this you can. Please check out the documentation at `http://www.splunk.com/` for instructions on this.

And we start the Splunk Forwarder on that machine:

`/opt/splunkforwarder/bin/splunk start`

 In Linux, starting or restarting Splunk in this way will start the command as the user you are currently logged in as, so if you need to start it as root, then `sudo` to root, and then start the Forwarder. Also, adjusting the `init.d` command to recognize Splunk is a best practice, and will enable the restarting of the Forwarder with the same user account as it was started with. To do this, just run `/opt/splunkforwarder/bin/splunk enable boot-start`.

Then just use `service splunk start/stop/restart` from the bash CLI.

Now that our Forwarder is up and running, and is pointed to our deployment server, we need to go to our Splunk UI to see if it's communicating effectively.

In our web browser we go to `http://mydeploymentserver.com:8089`, log in, and go to the menu as shown as in the following image:

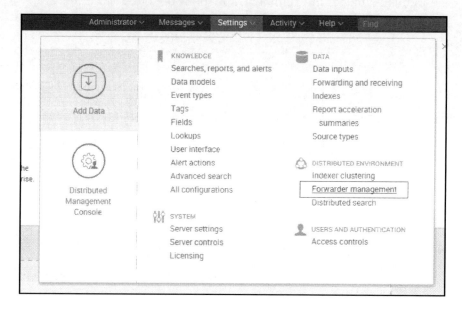

When we do so, we should see our client by both IP and hostname, communicating with our deployment server. If we don't, go to `/splunkforwarder/var/log/splunk/splunkd.log` on the Forwarder, as well as the `/splunk/var/log/splunk/splunkd.log` on the deployment server to troubleshoot.

When we see our host contacting our deployment server, we can then begin configuring it via the deployment server. First we need to create an app. An app is essentially a folder with a few files that have specific names in it.

In our case, we are going to use a custom script written by a Linux administrator to gather inventory metrics about a system.

This script uses a series of standard Linux system commands to gather the appropriate information and output in a Splunk-friendly format.

First, we need to create a folder in `/opt/splunk/etc/deployment-apps/`. I'm going to create a folder called `MyLinuxApp`.

Within `MyLinuxApp`, I'm going to create another folder called `local`, and one called `bin`. Within the local folder, I'm going to create a file called `inputs.conf`, and a file called `outputs.conf`.

So here are the files and folders we've created:

- `/opt/splunk/etc/deployment-apps/MyLinuxApp`
- `/opt/splunk/etc/deployment-apps/MyLinuxApp/bin`
- `/opt/splunk/etc/deployment-apps/MyLinuxApp/local`
- `/opt/splunk/etc/deployment-apps/MyLinuxApp/local/inputs.conf`
- `/opt/splunk/etc/deployment-apps/MyLinuxApp/local/outputs.conf`

This is now our new app.

Now, we need to put our script in the app. We will use a file transfer system to get the file there (WinSCP, SCP, Samba, or whatever you like), and when we get the `inventory.sh` script to our system, it will need to be put into the `/opt/splunk/etc/deployment-apps/MyLinuxApp/bin` folder.

So now, we have this in our deployment server:

- `/opt/splunk/etc/deployment-apps/MyLinuxApp`
- `/opt/splunk/etc/deployment-apps/MyLinuxApp/bin/inventory.sh`
- `/opt/splunk/etc/deployment-apps/MyLinuxApp/local`
- `/opt/splunk/etc/deployment-apps/MyLinuxApp/local/inputs.conf`
- `/opt/splunk/etc/deployment-apps/MyLinuxApp/local/outputs.conf`

Now we need to configure our app to use the `inventory.sh` script as a scripted input.

We need to go to `/opt/splunk/etc/deployment-apps/MyLinuxApp/local/inputs.conf` and add some settings.

In this file, we will add the following stanza, and configuration settings:

```
[script://./bin/inventory.sh]
interval =  604800
sourcetype = linux_inventory
source = inventory.sh
index = main
disabled = 0
```

The interval we set is in seconds, so this script will only run once a week. We will do this because we know that the inventory doesn't change very often, so a once a week update is all we need.

Now that we've created the data input, we need to adjust where this data will be sent. Remember that right now the Universal Forwarders that we are deploying in this app have no configuration at all, so we are going to configure them using this app.

We now need to adjust the `/opt/splunk/etc/deployment-apps/MyLinuxApp/local/outputs.conf` file.

To point to our indexer, so the data gets there from our Forwarders as expected, this configuration is placed in the `outputs.conf`:

```
[tcpout:myIndexer]
server = 10.10.10.10:9997
```

 Port `9997` is usually configured as a listener on indexers by default, but from time to time you will need to configure it. If it's not set up as a listening port, do so, or the data you send from your Forwarders will be lost. It's also not a bad idea to use DNS addresses in the `outputs.conf` as well if possible. The reasons are the same as using one for the deployment server.

Once we have our `inputs.conf` and `outputs.conf` configured, and our script in place within our app, we need to add a `serverClass` to our deployment server in order to tell it which machines to deploy to.

We will go to the `/opt/splunk/etc/system/local/serverclass.conf` file, and add some settings to do this.

The settings we will add will be these:

```
[serverClass:Linux]
whitelist.0 = MyLinuxEnvironment
[serverClass:Linux:app:MyLinuxApp]
```

Once we have adjusted these settings, it's time to reload the deployment server and check our index for data.

On the deployment server, we run the following command:

```
/opt/splunk/bin/splunk reload deploy-server -class Linux
```

In this example, we are reloading a single class. This becomes much more important when you have 50 or 60 server classes and thousands of Forwarders you're managing. If you use the standard `/opt/splunk/bin/splunk`, reload the deployment server. The deployment server will reload *all* server classes. If you have multiple admins with their hands in the cookie jar, and safe work times for different systems, this gets ugly quickly without the `-class` switch.

The Splunk Forwarder on our target devices will run our script one time when it receives it, so we should see data from all hosts we've configured this way. It will then wait a week and run it again. When troubleshooting, it's often recommended to crank up the interval to say 60 seconds to make sure the script works as expected.

In this example, we have created a working and auto-updating inventory of our Linux environment. We can run a search query to table all of the data by fields, and we can create pivots and forms to filter the data as people see fit on their reports.

Now that we've seen how to create and deploy a data input leveraging the deployment server, let's take a closer look at the other kinds of data inputs, shall we?

Know your data

Before you ever ingest a new data file with Splunk, it's wise to spend a few extra minutes putting that data into a test environment first to see how it will look. Sometimes, the files will be nicely formatted with a timestamp at the front of each event, and Splunk will suck it in and plot it in time very easily. The reason for this is so that you know if, or how, you need to break your events, or extract your fields. Taking this time before you put data into Splunk can save you hours of work later on.

Q: What do I do when I have a `rotating.out` log that is 3 GB in size, and constantly writes to the file? My Forwarder isn't sending everything in the file.
A: Use `crcSalt = <SOURCE>` on that file in `inputs.conf`.

The common reason can be that it's likely that Splunk isn't noticing the file change because of how far it looks ahead for new events in a file. When you add crcSalt, you ask Splunk to add a cyclic redundancy check on that file. Basically, you're asking Splunk to keep a constant eye on that file, and reingest whenever the Cyclic Redundancy Check mistmatch.

While adding a CRC is great, it also has a bit of a drawback. If your file does not have a timestamp at the beginning of each event, Splunk will pull in the whole file again.

Let's take an example with bash history files. If you're reading this book, you have a Linux server, so go cat the <home>.bash_history file in your Linux machine. Notice how there is no timestamp for the commands captured. That means when you add crcSalt to a file like this, a Forwarder will reingest the whole file because the Forwarder knows something has changed, effectively duplicating your data. Leave it on and well… dedup is all I have to say.

Long delay intervals with lots of data

This is another good example of when to use crcSalt. Let's say you have an admin-developed bash script that outputs 1.5 GB into a file every 30 minutes. Your user needs this data to scrub and create a report for your leaders. If you put a monitor stanza on that, you will likely not see any updates in Splunk after the initial ingestion.

While the best way is to simply analyze the admin workflow and move the data gathering to Splunk entirely, and then autogenerate the report in a dashboards panel, often there are things that prevent such occurrences. If you can, develop a script to poll the same data that your admin requires at an interval, and then offer them a dashboard with charted history. Leaders loves line graphs of history.

The reason is that Splunk only looks so far ahead in a file to see if things have changed, remember, so 1.5 GB is well beyond a Universal Forwarder's standard look ahead. Use crcSalt, and see if that resolves your issue.

The monitored input is probably the easiest to use within an environment. Here is a quick example of what one looks like:

```
[monitor:///opt/mapr-*/logs/*.log]
crcSalt = <SOURCE>
sourcetype = Hadoop_jobtrackerlogs
index = hadoop_joblogs
disabled = 0
```

There are a million other problems that can come up with a monitored input, and for those I would say check **Splunk Answers** (`https://answers.splunk.com/`) or the IRC channel. Each problem is unique, and those are great places to get some assistance.

Summary

In this chapter, we have discussed how to move on to understanding what kinds of data inputs Splunk uses in order to get data inputs. We have seen how to enable Splunk to use the methods which they have developed in data inputs. Finally, we have gained brief knowledge about the data inputs for Splunk.

In the next chapter, we will learn about how to format all incoming data to a Splunk-friendly format, pre-indexing, in order to ease search querying and knowledge management going forward.

3

Data Scrubbing

Getting data into Splunk can be a long process, and it is often a very important and overlooked process on a Splunk journey. If we do it poorly, there is lots of clean up that we have to do, which is usually much more complicated than just sitting down to plan out how we want our data to get to Splunk, and how we want it to look. This process is known as data scrubbing, or data cleaning. This is the process of breaking events at the proper line, as well as extracting some fields, or masking data before and after Splunk writes it to disk.

Topics that will be covered in this chapter:

- Heavy Forwarder management
    - What is a Heavy Forwarder?
    - Managing the deployment server
    - Installing modular inputs
- Data formatting
    - Event management
    - Knowledge management
- Pre/post indexing techniques to clean data before indexing
    - Pre-indexed field extractions
    - Data masking

We're going to focus on only a few pieces of a Splunk system in this chapter:

- Universal Forwarders
    - Thin clients that can be installed on a device
- Heavy Forwarders
    - Thick clients that can be installed on a device.
- Indexers
    - The data store for Splunk

The Universal Forwarder is the most popular forwarding tier to install on a machine and begin receiving data.

Heavy Forwarder management

A Heavy Forwarder is usually used in instances where an administrator needs some more functionality, such as event routing (errors go to the error index, and info messages go to the info index), data routing, or collecting API information to be sent to the indexers. Heavy Forwarders can also be used for advanced, detailed filtering of data to reduce indexing volume.

Indexers are the heart of a Splunk system, and you can think of them as a big database. They will almost always be the beefiest of your machines, because they are doing the lion's share of the heavy lifting.

This is a diagram depicting a typical Splunk deployment:

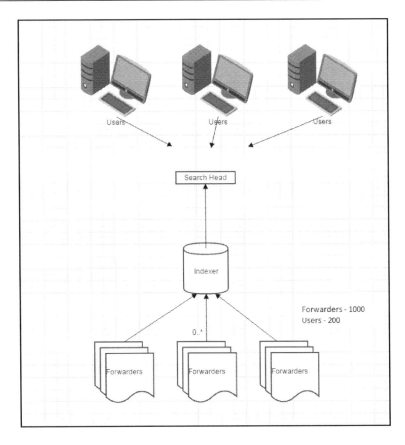

Within a Splunk deployment a new admin often asks the question: *When would you ever need a Heavy Forwarder?*

The answer to this question is complicated; however, I'll give a single use case where it is good to use a Heavy Forwarder.

A Heavy Forwarder should be deployed in circumstances in which data needs to be parsed, re-routed, consolidated, or *cooked* prior to delivering it to the indexer instead of merely forwarding raw data. Using a Heavy Forwarder can reduce the processing load on Splunk indexers. It can also perform more granular event filtering, reducing the overall data ingest. Finally, using a Heavy Forwarder to cook data allows us to transform inbound data, performing actions such as the obfuscation of fields before that data hits an indexer.

If a Splunk deployment looks like the preceding diagram, then the single **Indexer** is doing a lot of work. It's writing data to a disk rapidly, as well as answering search queries, and the **Search Head** is also under a lot of stress from all the **Users** trying to query things.

If someone wants to add API inputs to this architecture, it would be advisable to introduce a Heavy Forwarder to this architecture.

This is so you don't overwork either your **Indexer** or your **Search Head** by adding the API input to what they are doing, and reducing the user experience:

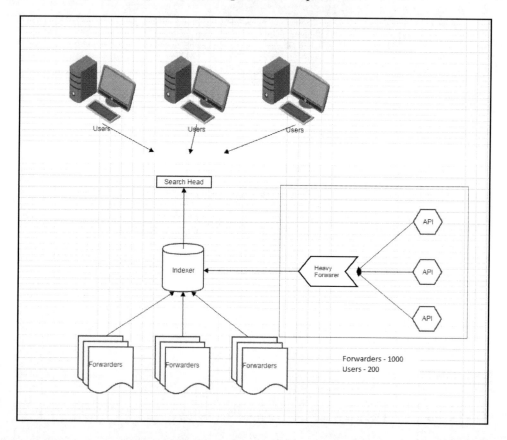

Adding the Heavy Forwarder to your configuration will take the load off querying the API and cooking the data, so your search head doesn't have to do the queries and the indexer doesn't have to cook the data.

It is also used as a consolidation point for data collection in a lot of architecture; that is, the Heavy Forwarder collects data for active directories, exchange networks, API's, and other sources, and cooks the data and sends it to the indexers.

The next question that is often asked is: H*ow do I install a Heavy Forwarder?*

Here are the steps (it's really easy):

1. Get a new machine.
2. Go to `http://www.splunk.com/`.
3. Download Splunk (the full version), and install it on your new machine.
4. Set the license from trial to forwarder.
5. Configure its `outputs.conf` to send data to your indexers:

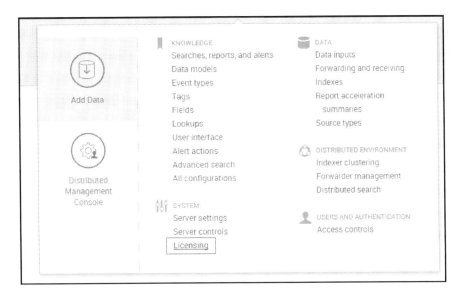

6. First go to **Settings | Licensing**:

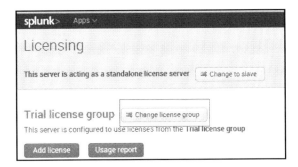

7. Then change the license group to **Forwarder license**:

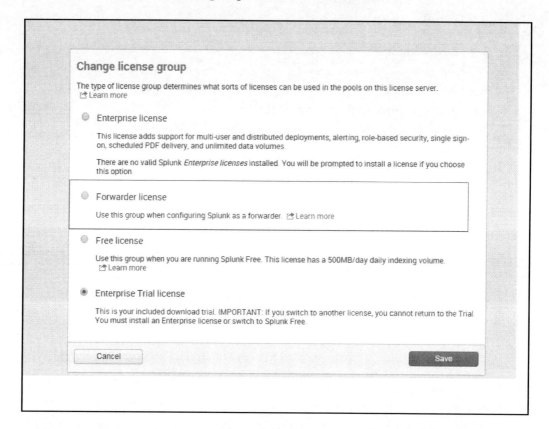

 When you do this, you will no longer have to use a username to login to this machine. If you need authentication, you will have to use an enterprise license.

8. Then go into **Forwarding defaults** and make sure you check **No** on the **Store a local copy of forwarded events?** section.
9. Go to **Forwarding and receiving**:

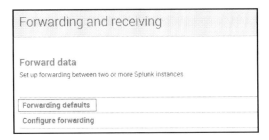

10. Then click on **Forwarding defaults** and check **No** on **Store a local copy of forwarded events?**

And like magic, you have a Heavy Forwarder.

Managing your Heavy Forwarder

There are two ways to manage a Heavy Forwarder:

- Manual administration
- Deployment server

Manual administration

Manual administration simply needs more effort, and is much less scalable. If you only have one Heavy Forwarder, then this may be the choice for you, but when you spin up four or five Heavy Forwarders it's a lot of effort to configure and manage them manually.

Deployment server

The Splunk deployment server is usually the preferred way to manage a large scale Splunk Forwarder deployment, as it is a central point of administration for both Universal and Heavy Forwarders. Setting this up is very easy.

In the file `deploymentclient.conf`, set the following settings:

```
[deployment-client]
disabled = 0

[target-broker:deploymentServer]
targetUri = <deploymentserver>:<managmentport>
```

Then restart the Splunk service, and check your deployment server list of Forwarders for the machine you installed it on.

Important configuration files

You will need to create a new app for your Heavy Forwarder in the `deployment-apps` directory of your deployment server, and then a couple of files:

- `outputs.conf`: Tells the Forwarder which indexers to connect to
- `props.conf`: This is where configurations for extractions and so on go
- `transforms.conf`: This is where we configure our masking (if needed)

Then after we create these files and configure our outputs, we simply add the new app, whitelist the hostname in `serverclass.conf` of the deployment server in `etc/system/local`, and reload the appropriate server class to distribute the app.

After you do this, make sure that you see the package deployed within the deployment server's UI to that host:

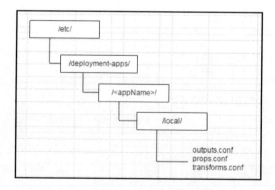

You are now managing your Heavy Forwarder with the deployment server.

Even data distribution

In most cases, the data distribution of every Forwarder is handled automatically within any Forwarder; however in some instances it is necessary to tell Splunk to force appropriate data distribution across the indexing layer. This is especially necessary when dealing with extremely large events and multiple indexing peers.

Let's take a clustered environment as an example:

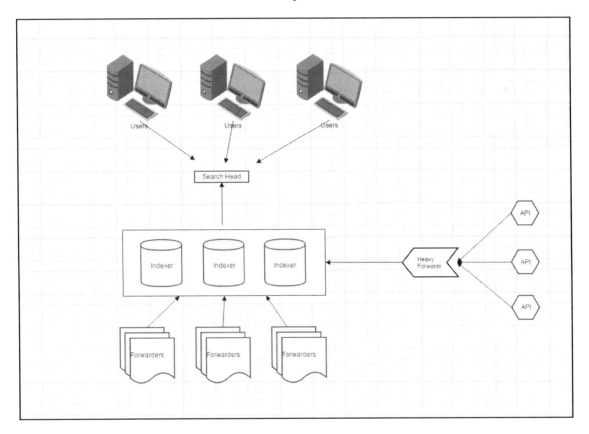

Let's say that two of our API's are pulling data from systems that have events in excess of 10,000 lines per event, and they are updating pulling this data at 60-second intervals.

While Splunk can certainly do this, and a Heavy Forwarder can handle the data throughput, there are a few settings that need to be in place to make sure not only that performance is optimized, but also that the data is being load-balanced properly, is not being truncated before the data can finish.

There are a few things to know when consuming very large datasets at fast intervals:

- By default, Splunk will only take in 1000 lines of an event
- By default, Splunk will not break an established TCP connection during data ingests
- By default, Splunk's throughput is set to a specific amount, and any data being sent to an indexer above that amount will be buffered in memory

For a Splunk admin, this results in a few inevitable outcomes if we don't manipulate the settings to accommodate our data set. These match the preceding list in terms of sequence:

- Our events will not be complete, and Splunk will drop the remainder of the data after truncation.
- If our data flow is constant with large events, the TCP connection will never stop, sending all data to a single indexer in a cluster. This results in a very large reduction in search performance.
- If left unchecked, this can consume all memory on the client device, resulting in system lock.

For our first instance, we have to go back through the events we are consuming, and do a cross-comparison of a full event versus a truncated event.

 The easiest way to identify Splunk truncation of a log is to view an event in Splunk and look for the timestamp in a very large event. If the event is being truncated, and your very large event starts with a timestamp, you will notice that the timestamp is not the first string of the event in Splunk.

So basically, in the preceding example we are looking at less than half of the event being on a single indexer, and potentially consuming the majority of the memory on the box.

This is what the above type of behavior may look like in a clustered Splunk environment:

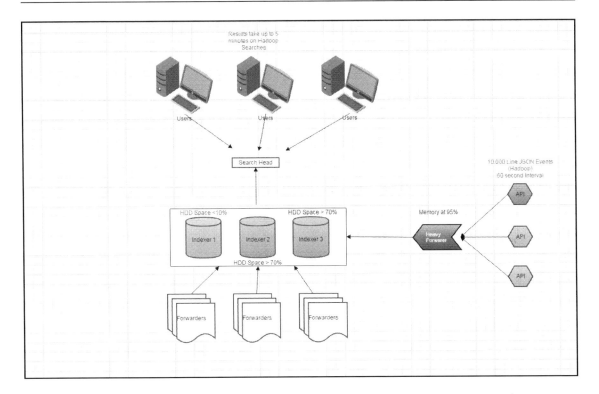

This event actually did occur in a real-time enterprise setting with one of the largest Hadoop infrastructures in the world. The infrastructure has over 2000 nodes, sometimes allocating more than 200,000 mappers to a single job. We were collecting all of the job counters per job and sending them to Splunk to analyze and report on, and we ran up to 600,000 jobs a day. If you're ever wondering if the data is too big for Splunk, let me give you an example of what is actually in place and working right now.

For anyone who doesn't know Hadoop, this is what that means. There was an API created to rewrite the data into JSON and give each mapper four basic counters. The job itself had around 12. Now let's do some math:

(Up to 200,000 mapers per job) * (4 counters per mapper) + (12 counters for the job itself) = 800,012 lines per job

So we were writing up to 800,012 lines into Splunk in real time, somewhere between 500,000 and 600,000 times a day… from a single cluster.

Now let's discuss how this issue can be fixed in your environment.

Common root cause

So, in the above example, we are getting complaints from our users about not only searches being slow, but also about the results being inaccurate on the Hadoop system. To a Splunk admin this is quite general, so in the preceding example, this is how we fixed the issue.

Our users were experiencing truncation of events, making the data inaccurate and unusable; however, we were also seeing a huge hit on our indexing tier on two indexers, and our Heavy Forwarder had almost no memory to operate, making it very slow even logging into the system. We saw all of the symptoms in the preceding diagram in our environment.

To fix this we added the following settings to our Heavy Forwarder and our Indexing tier in order to remediate the truncation issue:

```
props.conf

[mysourceType]
TRUNCATE = 0
MAX_EVENTS = 0
```

This allowed large events to not be truncated; however this slowed down viewing the events in raw format or in Verbose format in Splunk, and didn't solve our other two issues.

The memory issue on the Heavy Forwarder turned out to be a queueing issue, as the events were so large that Splunk had to place un-indexed events into memory, effectively consuming the machine's memory as the events were in real time.

To remediate this issue, we simply increased the throughput size that Splunk could send at a single time. This is set in the `limits.conf` of the Heavy Forwarder:

```
limits.conf

[thruput]
maxKBps = 10,000
```

 Make sure that the NIC on your device and on your indexer can handle the amount of throughput you are configuring. In our case, we had 10 Gbps NIC.

This prevented the Heavy Forwarder from queuing excess data in memory and waiting to send it to the indexer.

Knowledge management

The last thing we had to do was to make sure the Heavy Forwarder didn't just place all of the data on a single indexer within the cluster. We needed to load-balance the data equally across all of our indexers, which also increased search performance.

We did this by adding the following settings to the Heavy Forwarders `outputs.conf` file:

```
outputs.conf
[tcpout:myOutput]
forceTimebasedAutoLB = true
```

What this setting does is effectively force the Heavy Forwarder to break the TCP connection with the indexer it is currently writing to, and send data to another indexer, even if the Forwarder is still sending an event and hasn't broken the TCP connection to the indexer.

It's advisable to set the `forceTimebasedAutoLB = true` setting on all Forwarders, both Heavy and Universal, in order to evenly spread data across all indexers in a cluster. This way load balancing will take place no matter what data input you add, or how large or small it is.

The final thing we had to do was make sure that the Search Head was capable of at least attempting to render these large events. Keep in mind that in this case Splunk is limited by the browser you're using and how well it renders XML.

We added the following setting to our search heads `limits.conf` file:

```
limits.conf
max_mem_usage_mb = 10000
```

Please use common sense here. If your search head does not have 10 GB of memory, do not set the memory usage for each search to 10000. Set this setting to something feasible for your system, or upgrade the machine that you have to include more memory.

At the end of the day, we ended up with a dataset that was extremely large, being ingested by Splunk in real time and reported on a daily basis. This was something new, even to the people at Splunk, because of the sheer volume of data.

The following diagram attempts to convey how to optimize large datasets in your environment based on the example we just walked through:

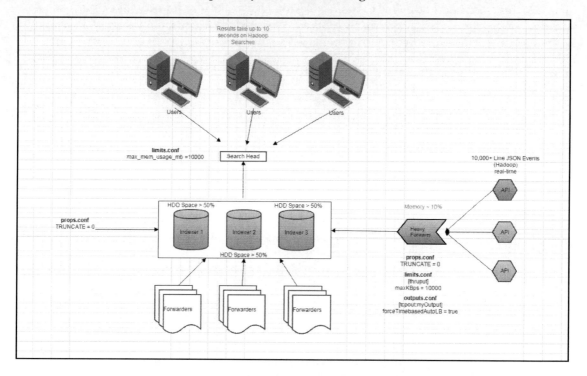

Handling single- versus multi-line events

By default, Splunk will use automatic line breaking to quantify events. Best practices state that depending on the type of events you have in your file, you should explicitly set your indexers appropriately. To do that, simply set this setting on your indexers `props.conf` appropriately:

```
SHOULD_LINEMERGE = true/false
```

Usually single-line events are quite easy for Splunk to handle; it's multi-line events that get a bit more complicated.

Time can be a tricky thing within each log type as well. In order to

As long as the timestamp is at the beginning of each event, then generally Splunk doesn't have much of a problem recognizing and breaking events around each timestamp.

Manipulating raw data (pre-indexing)

There are some advantages and disadvantages to using a Heavy Forwarder to deliver cooked data to the indexer. The primary advantage this gives us is better performance at search time. If we extract fields and break events before we write to disk, then it's less resource-intensive on the search head, and the indexer at search time.

The primary disadvantage only comes when we do these instances on the indexer itself, instead of offloading these types of operation to a Heavy Forwarder. The indexer will have to work harder to scrub the data before it writes it to disk, if a Heavy Forwarder is not the intermediary.

Routing events to separate indexes

Now that we have our Heavy Forwarder, we can start collecting data. In the first case, let's use a shared firewall file, to which multiple devices write their logs.

On Linux, it's pretty easy to add the shared mount to our Heavy Forwarder, and then we can just configure our Heavy Forwarder to ingest that file. That is a single `[monitor://]` stanza within our `inputs.conf` of our new Heavy Forwarder app in the deployment server. Let's assume we have done that.

So we are taking in some log files and the events are being broken just fine, and the data looks pretty clean.

We now have a new requirement for sending **intrusion** type events to the `infosec` index for the SOC, and then all standard events to our `firewall_logs` index.

This is where you will need a Heavy Forwarder, because we are now starting to organize our data at the event level by system and priority, and the Universal Forwarder does not have this functionality.

Here is a screenshot of the log events we want to send to our `infosec` index:

```
root@INTERNET-ROUTER> show log idp-log
Dec  3 06:57:46  INTERNET-ROUTER RT_IDP: IDP_ATTACK_LOG_EVENT: IDP: at 1354543066, SIG Attack log <192.168.1.102/63
279->63.245.215.56/21> for TCP protocol and service SERVICE_IDP application NONE by rule 1 of rulebase IPS in polic
y idp-pol-1. attack: repeat=0, action=CLOSE, threat-severity=INFO, name=custom-ftp, NAT <68.144.56.81:41248->0.0.0.
0:0>, time-elapsed=0, inbytes=0, outbytes=0, inpackets=0, outpackets=0, intf:TRUST:vlan.192->INTERNET:fe-0/0/0.0, p
acket-log-id: 0 and misc-message -

root@INTERNET-ROUTER>
```

These events are written to the shared firewall log we are currently ingesting. We need to use `props.conf` or `transforms.conf` in our Heavy Forwarder for this.

In our Heavy Forwarder, we can manipulate the raw data to route to separate indexes. We just need to create the appropriate settings and make sure we reference them properly.

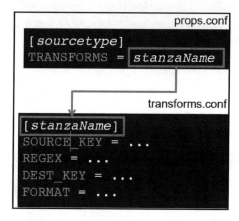

- **SOURCE_KEY** indicates which data to use as the source
- **REGEX** is the matching pattern we use to match our string in the data
- **DEST_KEY** is the setting that tells Splunk where to write the data
- **FORMAT** (optional): This is used to control how Splunk writes the data after it's matched

Make sure to specify your index for your new transform. In our instance, the settings would look like this:

```
props.conf
[firewall_logs]
TRANSFORMS = infosec
```

In order to do that, we need to adjust our `props.conf` and `transforms.conf` to separate indexing for the routing events:

```
Transforms.conf
[infosec]
REGEX = IDP_ATTACK_LOG_EVENT
DEST_KEY = _MetaData:Index
FORMAT = infosec
```

When we restart the Splunk Heavy Forwarder, we will see data begin appearing in the `infosec` index.

Black-holing unwanted events (filtering)

Let's take another example of when to manipulate raw data.

In this example, we have an SQL cluster that we are monitoring the Windows event logs on in order to see any issues that may be occurring. The SQL server uses AD authentication, which means any account authentication (service account or user) is tracked in the Windows event log.

While this may be something security people want to see, on a heavily utilized SQL database the volume of these kinds of events is tremendous, and is often not very useful to developers.

 For tracking authentication failures in Windows, it's much less cumbersome to track them through active directory. Installing the AD app for Splunk and the corresponding add-ons will pull in the appropriate data.

For our purpose, none of our users have any use for this data, so it's unused data that is counting against our license excessively and we're trying not to hit the license cap.

The way to stop this from happening while still ingesting the rest of the Windows event logs is to black-hole those events, also known as event filtering.

Remember that we are manipulating our Heavy Forwarder from the deployment server, so the `props` / `transforms` we must adjust are in our `<deployment-app-name>` on the deployment server. If we go to that location and we manipulate our configuration, `props.conf` and `transforms.conf` will look similar to this:

```
props.conf

[WinEventLog:System]
TRANSFORMS = black_hole
```

In order to do that, we need to adjust our `props.conf` and `transforms.conf` in pre-filtering for our pre-indexing:

```
transforms.conf

[black_hole]
REGEX = (?m)^EventCode=4624
```

```
DEST_KEY = queue
FORMAT = nullQueue
```

When we reload our deployment server, the deployment app with the new settings in the `props.conf` and `transforms.conf` files will be distributed to the client(s) in our `serverclass.conf`, and we will stop seeing the events with `EventCode=4624` authentication events in our data. As a side effect, our license will gain the extra headroom too, because we have stopped consuming those events.

Masking sensitive data

Masking data usually needs to happen when dealing with security or compliance. Generally speaking, HIPAA and PII (PCI) data are two very common instances where data needs to be masked before a Splunk user can see it. This is good for an employee on the phone running searches in Splunk and looking for account information, but they don't need anything but the last four digits of the card to search on.

Credit card information is usually the most common instance of this for Splunk, as credit card information can sometimes be seen in web application logs, so we will use that information in the next few pages.

There are two ways to mask this kind of data and, depending on your security and compliance regulations, you can use either depending on your policies:

 Consult your security and compliance department before implementing either of these in order to determine which method suits your needs best.

- **Pre-index data masking**: This means the data is replaced before it is actually written to disk, so there are no actual CC numbers within the Splunk Indexer
- **Search time data masking**: The data is written to disk in its raw form, so the sensitive data does exist in its original state on the Splunk Indexer

In most instances, the pre-index data mask is the most compliant, as it leaves no sensitive data on disk, and we can still run searches on all transactional data, or monitor data for system integrity.

Pre-index data masking

We will need our Heavy Forwarder to perform this action, so we will need to route data to the Heavy Forwarder first, before data reaches an indexer.

Let's say that we have all of our CC information in a single log file called `purchase_history.log` on each of our web servers, and they all hold this log in the same directory `/opt/data/secure/purchase_history.log`.

Within that log the data looks like this:

```
[01/15/2015:10:22:34] VendorID=44562 ccn:4556727302463532 purchaseCode=G
[01/15/2015:10:25:20] Send to checkout
txid=492ed69b-626f-48e1-8f79-29e94d27bd72
[01/15/2015:10:31:48] VendorID=67834 ccn:4929800800059530 purchaseCode=A
```

As you can see, above our `ccn` is our credit card number for each transaction on our system. We want to "x" out all of the numbers except the last four of the CC number, so that our Splunk users don't have access to this information.

Leveraging our deployment server, we would deploy the following configurations to this data and leverage the `SEDCMD` function of Splunk:

```
props.conf
[source:::///opt/data/secure/purchase_history.log]
SEDCMD-ccnmask = s/ccn=\d{12}(\d{4}.*)/ccn=xxxxxxxxxxxx\1/g
```

This will effectively replace the first 12 digits of the CC with a lowercase "x", and then the Heavy Forwarder will forward this to the indexer.

> This is also very useful in masking trade information for any major financial institution while still allowing transactional analysis for development and operations.
>
> This method is *destructive* to your data set, meaning that once it's written to disk this way, there is no way to restore any of that data. The data that is being masked is simply lost.

Post-index data masking

For this example, we will use the same data and the same use case; however, we will simply say that our security department doesn't have the same rules of compliance with this use case.

In this case, this data will be going on the search head of our architecture, so that we can mask the data at search time. We do this through a query, so the only thing that is being changed is the data at search time. If a user was to | `table _raw`, they would still see the underlying CC information.

This method is not destructive, but depending on the privileges of the Splunk roles you've created and the data you want them to see, this can cause a bit more administrative overhead.

In older versions of Splunk you can use transforms for this functionality. For more information on anonymizing data using a transform, check out this link: `http://docs.splunk.com/Documentation/Splunk/6.2.8/Data /Anonymizedatausingconfigurationfiles`.

When we search for our information we see it in its raw form, which looks like this:

We still see the full number within the data. To hide this data, simply add an `eval` statement with a `replace` function:

```
eval ccn=replace(ccn,"(\d{12})(\d{4})","XXXXXXXXXXXX\2") | table _time
VendorID ccn purchaseCode
```

When we do that, we start to see the mask we have been looking for:

This is best used in saved dashboards where users do not have the privileges to change or drilldown on this data. In many cases, it's good to create a summary index of this information to improve performance, as well as enhance the security of sensitive data.

Setting a hostname per event

This technique comes in handy when there is a large log that always prints a host name within the file; however, it's being consumed by a consolidated server, such as a Heavy Forwarder.

There are two ways to do this:

1. Configure the Heavy Forwarder to manipulate the underlying host field metadata and rewrite it with the new value.
2. Extract a new field and call it anything else besides host. Hostname usually works here.

The advantage of the first option is that we're overwriting data before its index, so we won't impact search head performance by extracting a new field and then searching on it. That will be the method we are focusing on here.

This is our dataset:

```
[02/24/2016:01:02:55 transaction accepted rcv_host=server12 txid=
1fd02dff-83f8-47ab-8b35-bc0b539eee09
[02/24/2016:01:04:21 transaction rejected rcv_host=server02 txid=
fdb9daa3-73de-4761-8bda-09e9c80090de
[02/24/2016:01:010:11 transaction accepted rcv_host=server01 txid=
ea629995-3803-4347-a535-50a9f90636a0
```

And this comes from sales.log on our Heavy Forwarder that has access to the file share being used to write to this file:

```
props.conf
[sales_logs]
TRANFORMS-rcvHosts = rcv_host
```

In order to do that, we need to adjust our props and transforms in the deployment server app for our Heavy Forwarder:

```
transforms.conf
[rcv_host]
REGEX = rcv_host=(\w+)
DEST_KEY = MetaData:Host
FORMAT = host::$1
```

When we adjust this on our Heavy Forwarder and restart the service, we will begin seeing the host name being replaced with the value of the rcv_host field within the logs.

Summary

In this chapter, we have discussed how to format all incoming data to a Splunk-friendly format, pre-indexing in order to ease search querying and knowledge management going forward.

In the next chapter, we will discuss how to create events, fields, saved searches, and metadata (permissions) on the data ingested. We will also discuss the importance of each knowledge object, the best practices, and importance of knowledge object creation and management.

4
Knowledge Management

In this chapter we are going to learn some techniques to manage incoming data in your Splunk indexers, some basics on how to leverage those knowledge objects to enhance performance when searching, as well as the pros and cons of pre- and post-field extraction.

Now that we've learned how to get all of our data into Splunk in effective ways, the next question is *How can I search for what I want?* That is a loaded question with Splunk, because any ninja out there will answer that with the question, *What do you want to see?*

Understanding the basics of the search syntax, as well as search behavior, is a great way of understanding why you need to create events, fields, and lookups. Have you ever been to a Splunk event, seen people just clicking away at dashboards and noticed how smoothly it operates? That's because for weeks prior to an event people are behind the scenes building knowledge objects to make everything flow smoothly during a presentation. They create lots of knowledge objects and lookups to ease the searching process, and then they form a well-structured search and save it to a dashboard or as a data model so the data renders quickly.

Anatomy of a Splunk search

There are three basic components to a Splunk search, and all of them have an effect on how quickly the data itself is rendered in your search panel.

Root search

This is the portion of the search that defines where the data itself is located within Splunk. It consists of any one of the four core Splunk fields. Index, sourcetype, source, and host are the core Splunk fields that can only be aliased; it usually not advisable to write them.

Calculation/evaluation

This is the portion of the search where we leverage some statistical functions, eval functions, or multi-value field functions in order to prepare the data we are searching for and the way we want to present it. The order of functions is very critical in this section of the query and is usually the largest portion of a search.

Presentation/action

This is the portion of the search where we present our search in either a chart or a table, and we let Splunk render the data as we asked it to. This is the last portion of any search and it directly affects how the data is presented to the end user. It can also perform an action, such as running a script.

Following is a search broken down into these three components:

```
Index=myIndex sourcetype=was:pids earliest_time=0 latest_time=now()
|rex "(?<pid>\d+)"
|stats latest(pid) as pid by jvm_server,host
|join type=inner jvm_server [search index="myIndex" earliest_time=-15m latest_time=now()
sourcetype="iis" website="*" host=host1 OR host=host2 OR host=host3 OR host=host4 OR host=host5
sc_status=5*| lookup status_codes.csv status AS sc_status | rename sc_status AS status | eval
uri=lower(cs_uri_stem)| search uri=*.do|stats count,latest(_time) as Latest_Alert_Time by host
uri|rex field=uri "\/(?<jvm_server>.*?)\/.*"|dedup jvm_server sortby - Latest_Alert_Time |eval
jvm_server=jvm_server."_server"|fields jvm_server,Latest_Alert_Time|search NOT [|inputlookup
Killed_Processes.csv|where return_code==0|fields jvm_server,Latest_Alert_Time]]
|fields host,pid,jvm_server,Latest_Alert_Time
|eval user="privUser"
|eval command="/usr/local/bin/sudo kill ".pid
|callsshscript host=host user=user command=command
|eval Status=if(return_code==0,"Successfully Killed","Failed")
|outputlookup Killed_Processes.csv
```

You can see that the first **root search** section highlighted in red is not that long, as we are just giving it direction as to where the data we want is located.

The next section highlighted in blue is the calculation evaluation portion and is made up of the actions we are taking with that data, as well as reaching out to correlate other data within the Splunk system and adding a few fields.

The last section is the **presentation** section of our search query, which tells Splunk what to do with this data. In this case, we are running a script through a custom function written by a Splunk ninja to stop a specified service on a machine.

Best practices with search anatomy

There are three basic components of search anatomy. You will have a better working knowledge of search query syntax after reading the following information.

The root search

Always make sure to list as many metadata fields as you can in this section because that will speed up your search results. If you just put a `host=host2` call in this part of the search, Splunk will scrub every index, every sourcetype, and every source within your selected time-range for that host, which takes a lot longer than if you specify the data location you want. The proper use of this portion usually looks something like this:

```
index=MyIndex sourcetype=iisLogs source=".../inetpub/*.log" host=host1 OR
host=host2
```

This small action can reduce your search times significantly.

Calculation/evaluation

Because this portion of the search query is usually the longest, the order of operation is critical here, as well as calling out all necessary fields and passing them down to the next part of your calculation.

For instance, in this search:

```
index=os sourcetype=cpu | eval linuxCPU=100 - pctIdle | lookup
server_inventory.csv nix_host as host | rename linuxCPU as nixUtil |
stats sparkline(avg(linuxCPU)) as averagePCT avg(linuxCPU) as pctCPU by
host cores model | sort - pctCPU | eval pctCPU=round(pctCPU.2) | eval
pctCPU=(pctCPU + "% Used")
```

We can see that the order is pretty crucial and that, if we aren't passing our fields down to our underlying functions, we won't get any results.

Here, we are creating the field called `linuxCPU` from a mathematical function and also performing a lookup to get some server inventory information before we start averaging:

```
| eval linuxCPU=100 - pctIdle | lookup server_inventory.csv nix_host as
host
```

We then rename the field to something that a user can easily understand:

```
| rename linuxCPU as nixUtil
```

We then attempt to perform a | stats function and perform some averaging on the field, while breaking out the results with a split by clause into three fields: **host**, **cores**, and **model**:

```
| stats sparkline(avg(linuxCPU)) as averagePCT avg(linuxCPU) as pctCPU
by host cores model
```

This search won't work if we run it this way.

Nowhere within our statistical functions is there a nixUtil field. The stats function is still trying to reference the linuxCPU field that no longer exists because it has been renamed.

That being said, there are two ways to fix this:

1. Change the field name in all underlying functions.
2. Remove the **rename** function.

Once adjusted appropriately, our search now looks like this:

```
index=os sourcetype=cpu | eval linuxCPU=100 - pctIdle | lookup
server_inventory.csv nix_host as host | stats sparkline(avg(linuxCPU))
as averagePCT avg(linuxCPU) as pctCPU by host cores model | sort -
pctCPU | eval pctCPU=round(pctCPU,2) | eval pctCPU=(pctCPU + "% Used")
```

Presentation/action

When formatting data differently in order to present it to the user, always make sure the fields you are using are present and being passed down from all other proceeding functions.

Just like with the *Calculation/evaluation* section of our search:

```
index=os sourcetype=cpu | eval linuxCPU=100 - pctIdle | lookup
server_inventory.csv nix_host as host | stats sparkline(avg(linuxCPU))
as averagePCT avg(linuxCPU) as pctCPU by host cores model | sort -
pctCPU | eval pctCPU=round(pctCPU.2) | eval pctCPU=(pctCPU + "% Used")
```

This search will not work at presentation level either. The reason is the same, and this is the final query:

```
index=os sourcetype=cpu | eval linuxCPU=100 - pctIdle | lookup
server_inventory.csv nix_host as host | rename linuxCPU as nixUtil | stats
sparkline(avg(linuxCPU)) as averagePCT avg(nixUtil) as pctCPU by host cores
model | sort - pctCPU | eval pctCPU=round(pctCPU,2) | eval pctCPU=(pctCPU +
"% Used")
```

Knowledge objects

There are bunch of different types of knowledge object and different ways to use them in Splunk to make searching easier:

Knowledge Object	Description
Reports	Saved searches of specific data and visualizations
Alerts	Saved searches of specific data set to email an alert or commit an action when triggered
Events	A log string that is saved and given a name for later reference during a search query
Field extractions	Very specific values within a log event that can be extracted with regex; often things such as user or dest_addr
Tag	An ancillary category market for disparate yet similar event types/hosts/systems
Field alias	A second name given to a field within a sourcetype – for instance, user can be aliased to src_user
Lookups	Usually a .csv or KV store that enhances the integrity of the data being searched
Workflow actions	Usually a link to a URL or a POST action to gather data from another web source

Macro	A referenced series of functions of query syntax that can process arguments

Within these there are two or three fundamental knowledge objects that usually require constant attention from a Splunk administrator. They are as follows:

- **Event type**: Finds log strings that represent an action or a portion of a transaction. Often finds the string in the log that represents **user login** or **user logoff**.
- **Field Extraction**: Uses Regex to extract the appropriate values that are desired by the users, such as **user** or **src_addr**.
- **Lookups**: This is usually a `.csv` file created by a subject matter expert to enhance the data that is already in Splunk. For instance, IIS status code descriptions or Cisco error code descriptions.
- **Tags**: A flag you can add to any knowledge object. Usually a categorization of different knowledge objects.

Eventtype Creation

Event types are one of the fundamental building blocks within Splunk, and without them administration can become increasingly cumbersome and people won't be able to familiarize themselves with the events within a system. There are two different ways to create an event type within Splunk.

Creation through the Splunk UI

We can create an event type by leveraging the Splunk UI and simply saving the relevant events as an event type we create.

To do this, we must first have a root search for the event types we want to see. In this example, we will use Linux syslog data.

In our root search, you can see that we have started focusing on the data that we really want and that we have received all of the events that show Linux is preventing access to a device.

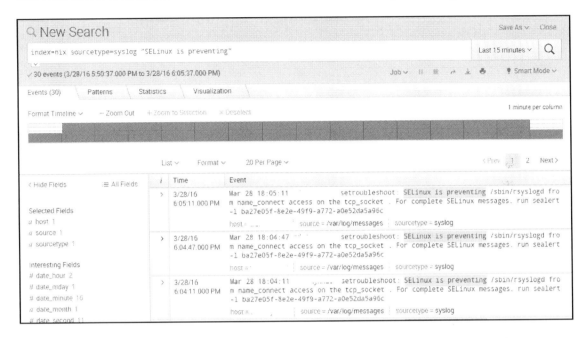

The next thing we can do, once we have the root search, is click on the **Save As** button in the top-right corner and click **Event Type**:

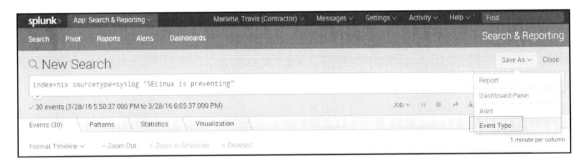

Now, when we do that, it will ask us how we want to name our event. With knowledge objects it is recommended to have a naming convention in order to find knowledge objects in the future with ease.

Please choose your naming convention carefully for knowledge objects. As your Splunk system grows, your knowledge objects will multiply exponentially.

After you have named your event, click **Save**. The other options are there if you care to tag, color-code, or adjust the priority of your event type.

Creation through the backend shell

When creating an event type through the shell, we still need to understand what the search is to narrow our results to only the events we want.

In this case, we will use the same search as before:

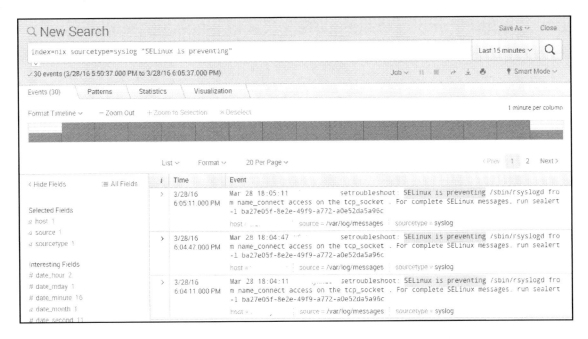

Once we have the search results, we use **PuTTY** to log in to the backend Linux host and add the event.

When we log in, we go to the `/opt/splunk/etc/apps` folder.

We then add the setting:

```
[myEventtype]
search = index=nix sourcetype=syslog "SELinux is preventing"
```

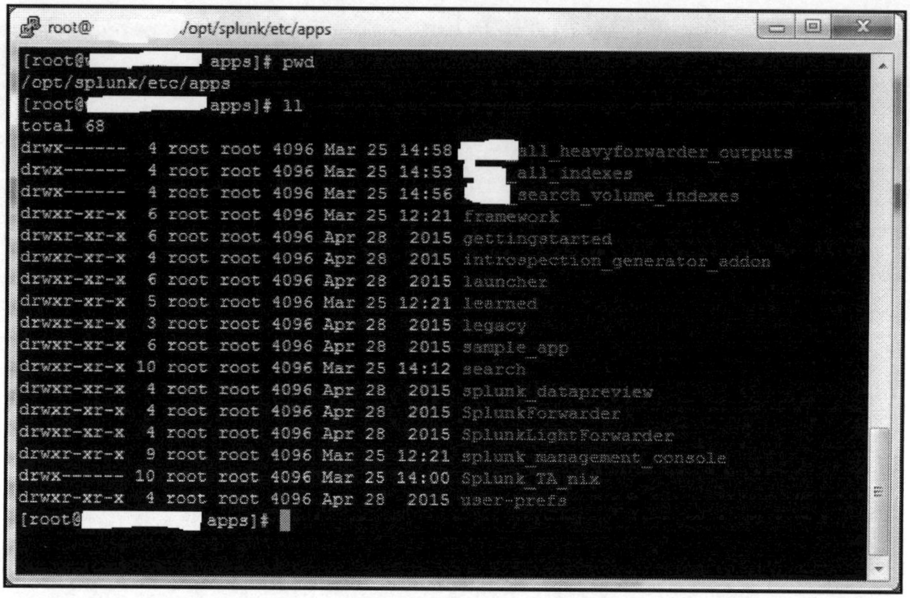

Once there, we can decide which app we want to put this in. In most cases, the default search app is adequate.

So, in /opt/splunk/etc/apps/search/eventtypes.conf, we place the following entry:

```
[myEventtype]
search = index=nix sourcetype=syslog "SELinux is preventing"
```

This looks like the following screenshot:

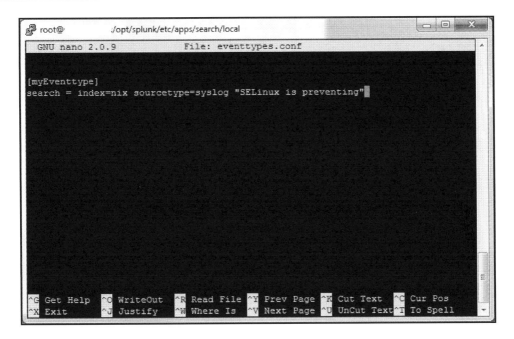

We then run the command in the browser to debug/refresh and wait for Splunk to reload its configurations; then, we are ready to use our event type in our search query.

Before going on to field extractions, would this be a good place to reference the capability of leveraging Splunk as a development platform? After pointing out the ability to run searches via the command line, it might be good to at least include a link to Splunk's SDK materials:

```
http://dev.splunk.com/view/get-started/SP-CAAAESB
```

```
← → C ⌂ 🔒 https://splunk:8000/en-US/debug/refresh
⠿ Apps  GitHub - Systems En...  C RAC  SolarWinds  Time / Expense  Splunk  Asana  M gmail

Entity refresh control page
===============================
'''
Forces a refresh on splunkd resources

        This method calls a splunkd refresh on all registered EAI handlers that
        advertise a reload function.  Alternate entities can be specified by appending
        them via URI parameters.  For example,

            http://localhost:8000/debug/refresh?entity=admin/conf-times&entity=data/ui/manager

        will request a refresh on only 'admin/conf-times' and 'data/ui/manager'.

        1) not all splunkd endpoints support refreshing.
        2) auth-services is excluded from the default set, as refreshing that system will
           logout the current user; use the 'entity' param to force it
...

Refreshing admin/conf-times            OK
Refreshing data/ui/manager             OK
Refreshing data/ui/nav                 OK
Refreshing data/ui/views               OK
Refreshing admin/alert_actions         OK
Refreshing admin/citrix_netscaler      OK
Refreshing admin/clusterconfig         OK
Refreshing admin/clustersearchheadconfigOK
Refreshing admin/collections-conf          BadRequest
 In handler 'collections-conf': Must use user context of 'nobody' when interacting with collection configurations {used user='admin'}
Refreshing admin/commandsconf          OK
Refreshing admin/conf-deploymentclient OK
Refreshing admin/conf-inputs           OK
Refreshing admin/conf-times            OK
Refreshing admin/conf-wmi              OK
Refreshing admin/connections           OK
Refreshing admin/cooked                OK
Refreshing admin/datamodel-files       OK
Refreshing admin/datamodelacceleration OK
Refreshing admin/datamodeledit         OK
Refreshing admin/deploymentserver      OK
Refreshing admin/dispatch              OK
Refreshing admin/eventtypes            OK
```

Field extractions

Field extractions are values within a log event that we wish to see as part of our results when we search. The most common fields are usually things such as **user** or **src_ip**, but as long as we can use RegEx well, we can extract pretty much anything.

There are many ways to create a field extraction within Splunk; however I am only going to focus on two different ways to extract fields and two examples of when to do so.

Performing field extractions

There are two occasions where we can perform field extractions for Splunk, and there are pros and cons for both.

Pre-indexing field extractions (index time)

Pre-indexed field extractions are when we extract fields from our desired data set *before* we write the data to disk. This is usually done on either a heavy forwarder or an indexer before data is sent to the Indexers to write:

- Pros:
    - Increases performance at search time
- Cons:
    - Destructive write to disk
    - Consumes resources on device (Indexer/Heavy Forwarder)
    - High administrator overhead

It is recommended that this type of extraction is only used if the search heads are over-utilized in their running state. If this type of extraction must be done, then make sure that you are extracting the data from *every* event type you want before you write it to disk. There is no going back once you write this data to disk, unless you clean the index itself.

Post-indexing field extractions (search time)

Search time field extractions are the most common way to extract value from your data. This type of extraction can be done in the query bar with a `rex` command or in `props.conf` and `transforms.conf`. Splunk also has an easy interface that can be used when performing this type of operation called the **Interactive Field Extraction** (**IFX**) tool. This tool is pretty easy to use, although there are things that it will miss no matter how hard you try. It's better to simply learn RegEx itself and make your own extractions.

- Pros:
    - Ease of use
    - Flexibility of operation
    - Low administrative overhead
    - Non-destructive
- Cons:
    - Can affect search performance negatively for users when the volume of extractions reaches thousands of fields

It's highly recommended that you use search time field extractions not only due to their flexibility, but also their non-destructive nature. If you mess up your RegEx, you can simply change it and Splunk will just pull out the new value while reading data from the indexers.

Creating index time field extractions

We cannot use the UI to create an index time field extraction. We must use a series of `props.conf` and `transforms.conf` settings in order to enable this type of extraction.

Let's take a `syslog` event and try it out.

Here's our data:

```
Mar 31 17:56:59 myHost postgres[13011]: [178005-1] postgres postgres
localhost 13011 2016-03-31 17:56:59 EDT SELECTLOG: duration: 0.435 ms
```

We want to extract the `duration` field from this data. There's a key question to ask before we extract this data.

Is the duration only measured in **MS** or does `ms` change values to minutes and hours dependant on actual duration?

The answer to that question will adjust your RegEx considerably and may make the extraction itself next to impossible. For our case, let's say that this field is always measured in `ms`.

First, we need to make sure that our extraction works, so we would use the RegExr tool to confirm that it matches what we want:

So, now that we have our extraction, we need to go to our indexer (or cluster master or heavy forwarder, depending on your architecture) and add that RegEx to our `Transforms.conf` under a new stanza:

```
Transforms.conf
[syslog_duration]
REGEX = duration:\s(?<duration>[^ ]+)
FORMAT = duration::"$1"
WRITE_META = true
```

After we have created this entry, we then need to call that transform from our `Props.conf` in the same folder, under the appropriate sourcetype stanza.

```
Props.conf
[syslog]
TRANFORMS-duration = syslog_duration
```

And finally, when we have set our `Props.conf` appropriately, we need to enable the indexer to actually write this field to disk itself. We do this with a setting in `fields.conf`, which will live in the same folder as the rest of these files. (Usually, that is `/opt/splunk/etc/apps/<appname>/local.`)

```
Fields.conf
[duration]
INDEXED = true
```

We will need to repeat these steps for all fields that require index time extractions.

Creating search time field extractions

We can create search time field extractions in a few different ways. We can use RegEx in the query bar, via a | `Rex` command, we can use the **interactive field extractor** (**IFX**), or lastly we can adjust `props.conf` / `transforms.conf` ourselves manually. There are likely more methods available, which other fellow Splunkers will remind me of, but here I will only focus on two ways of performing search time field extractions.

Creating field extractions using IFX

For this example, we are going to use syslog data and see if we can extract a field from it.

Here is a string from our data:

```
Mar 29 17:14:58 myHostName rsyslogd-2177: imuxsock begins to drop messages
from pid 31881 due to rate-limiting
```

In the previous example data , we want to extract the `pid` field using the UI. To do this, we click on the little arrow next to the event in Splunk and then select **Extract Fields** from the **Event Actions** menu:

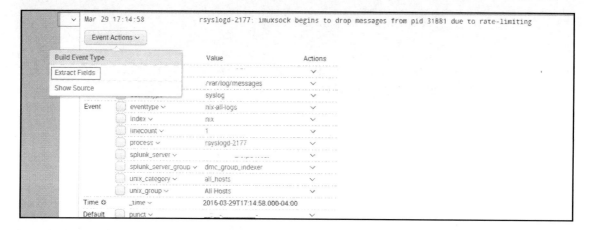

When we do that, Splunk takes us to the IFX tool that Splunk developed.

Here, we can highlight our desired field value, and Splunk will write a RegEx to match and extract that field for us:

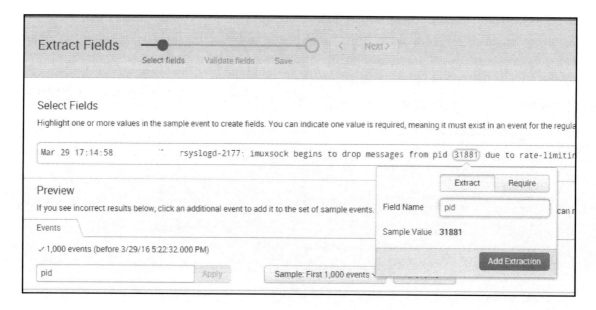

When you've highlighted the appropriate field value and named your field, you can click through the **Validate fields** and then finally to the **Save** part of the extraction process:

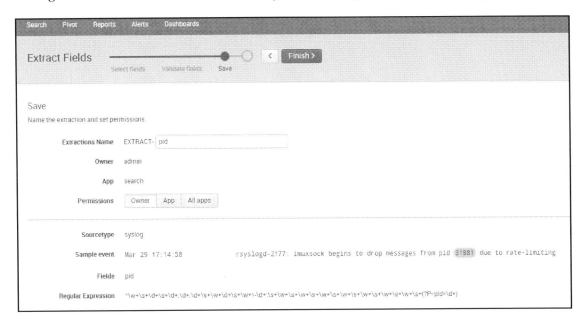

Here, you can see the long **Regular Expression** part of this section. This is the actual RegEx code you are using to extract the field.

It would be a good idea to point out where field extractions performed via the IFX are stored in Splunk. I often use the IFX as a first attempt at field extraction, which I then refine. It can be helpful to know where that original props is sitting in order to use it as a template, or make sure that I remember to delete it.

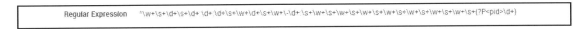

While sometimes Splunk's IFX works well, in some instances it is necessary to manually generate the field extractions, which takes someone who is highly proficient with RegEx.

If you are a Splunk admin and you're not familiar with RegEx, familiarize yourself as quickly as you can – you will need it.

Creation through CLI

Creating these through the CLI is a bit different, but often much more effective in extracting just the fields that you want. We will use the same previous example data, and instead of using the IFX we will copy this out to a web-based RegEx pattern matcher to extract our field.

We copy this data out:

```
Mar 29 17:14:58 myHostName rsyslogd-2177: imuxsock begins to drop messages
from pid 31881 due to rate-limiting
```

And paste it into the content box at `http://www.regexr.com/`.

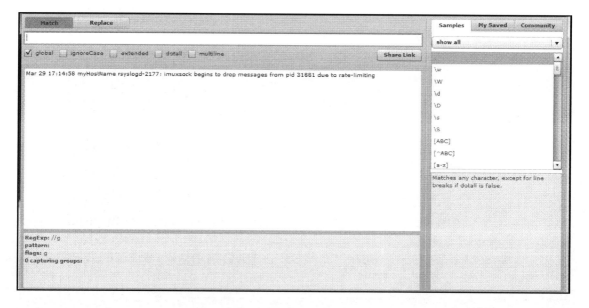

We begin writing our RegEx to match our desired field value and extract only the values we want. In this case, we will use the RegEx `pid\s(?<pid>\d+)`:

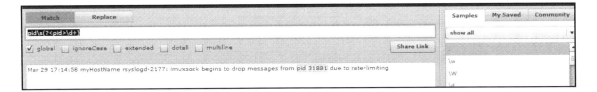

And we will then place that in the `props.conf` file in `/opt/splunk/etc/apps/search/` under the appropriate source type:

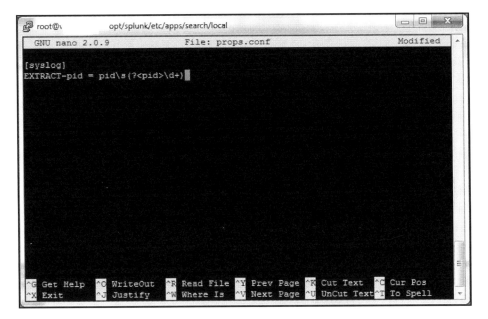

When we have placed that setting, we then do a soft refresh of the search head, like before; when it's done we will have our new field.

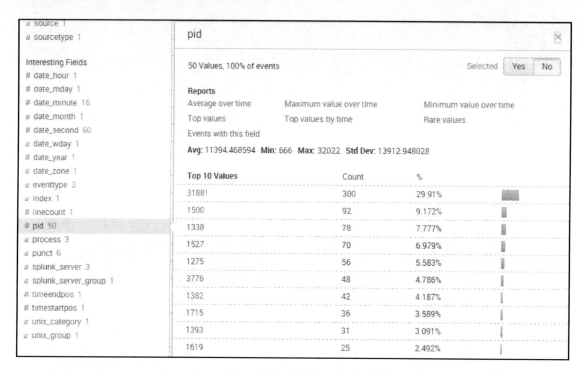

Summary

In this chapter, we have learned some techniques to manage the incoming data in your Splunk indexers; some basics on how to leverage those knowledge objects to enhance performance when searching; and the pros and cons of pre- and post-field extraction.

In the next chapter, we will discuss how to use these events and fields to create saved searches, reports, and alerts on the data ingested. I will also discuss some self-healing techniques within alerting, so you can begin automating some of your top workflows, such as restarting a hung service.

5
Alerting

Alerting is the act of getting a notification, let's say an SMS, email, or otherwise, to raise awareness to an outage or potential issue. Alerting itself has become more and more important within companies, and the alerting tools that are in place can be very expensive, expensive to scale, and very exclusive to specific systems. They also often don't offer as much intelligence within the alert, and they may not be as customizable as a tool like Splunk to the needs of a company. Every organization wants an alerting system that sends only actionable alerts and eliminates **noisy** alerts. Splunk can be good for consolidating multiple alerting tools, as well as reducing alert noise.

Alerting in Splunk is much more complex than just saving a search query. Where the action may be that easy, it is also a matter of understanding the fine details to explain what the alert is doing once you receive an actionable alert that makes the alert successful or not.

In this chapter we will learn about the following topics:

- Setting expectations (leadership)
  - Real-time
  - Be specific
  - Predictions
- Anatomy of an alert
  - Search query/results
  - Alert naming
  - Schedule
  - Trigger
  - Action
  - Throttling
  - Permissions
- Alert creation

- Creating custom commands/automated self-healing
- Splunk Custom Alert Framework (introduced with 6.3) `http://docs.splunk.co m/Documentation/Splunk/6.4.1/AdvancedDev/ModAlertsIntro`
- We will also cover the availability of a wide range of custom alerting apps on the Splunk base for platforms such as Jira, ServiceNow, and even Twitter `https://sp lunkbase.splunk.com/apps/#/page/1/search/alerts/order/relevance/cont ent/alert_actions`

Also, should there be at least some passing reference to the correlated alert capabilities in Splunk for ITSI and Splunk ES?

Setting expectations

I expect that every organization is different with respect to their criteria for what they are alerting on. However, I can tell you from working across many sectors, and at some major institutions, that leadership generally wants the same thing no matter what company you work for. Allow me to give you a breakdown list of what leaderships' expectations are of Splunk and its alerting capabilities, across industries.

Splunk should be able to:

- Alert on the future
- Predict the future
- Automatically know when all users are experiencing problems simultaneously
- Tame dragons
- Slay gods
- Perform prophetic-like miracles in real-time
- Save them billions of dollars
- Automate their departments' workflow

After all, it is a **Big Data** platform with **machine learning** capabilities, right?

I am exaggerating here, but Splunk is both a big data platform and one that has machine learning capabilities. Contrary to popular belief it is not SkyNet nor the Matrix. I've checked under the hood; I didn't see Arnold or Neo.

There are a few components of setting expectations that are often overlooked that I would like to cover, to ease your life before you, the administrator (a.k.a. the great and powerful Oz), becomes accountable for both magic and the future.

Time is literal, not relative

The concept of time has been a topic of discussion since early civilization. However, when it comes to enterprise alerting, it becomes a very real slip-stream of accountability. By this I mean that when SLAs are present, real-time costs money, and no one wants to be caught being accountable for breaching an SLA and costing their company money. The alerting system directly impacts a team's ability to be responsive, and, as Splunk is often used in monitoring, it assists in the finger-pointing game after money is lost.

Setting a real-time alert with a tool like Splunk could be exactly what the doctor ordered. It could also crash your outbound notification server (either SMTP or SMS) and shut down alerting for all of your systems.

Allow me to give you an example to explain.

I once had a member of my leadership ask me to set up a real-time alert on a system that bypassed QA and landed directly in production. The alert was going to be based on a long string that the developers had stated represented a catastrophic failure within the software log.

The logs we were monitoring at the time generated 12GB an hour, because what's better than testing in production? Why having the logger hard coded to DEBUG mode, of course!

I asked three questions before I set the alert because I'm a firm believer that if someone answers the same question the same way when asked three different ways, they are sure they want that outcome.

Here are the questions:

- What if we were to schedule an alert to check every 5 minutes?
    - Answer: No, we want it in real time.
- Are you sure you want real-time alerts? There could be a lot of them.
    - Answer: Of course we are sure.
- Will anyone actually react to alerts sent from an application logging them in nanoseconds?
    - Answer: If they don't react, then it's a problem for leadership. Our 24-hour staff should be reacting in real time as well.

You may be able to see why I started asking questions like this, and where I'm leading to, and I must say it was funny. Not for leadership, but certainly to observe.

I enabled the alert at 4 p.m., and I received a phone call from my executive at 10 p.m. screaming at me to turn off the alert and asking who authorized it.

The next day we had a discussion about real-time alerting again and he asked me why I hadn't mentioned that this was a possible outcome. I responded that I actually asked that question three times, and I showed him the email I sent to both him and his colleagues.

Apparently, a couple of members of leadership that were on the distribution group that Splunk was sending to were out to dinner with external colleagues, and all of the internal leaderships, phones started buzzing at the same time from the notifications.

The notifications, however, didn't stop. Splunk was sending 5,000 emails a minute to that email distribution group, and the members that were at dinner couldn't access their phones because the phones were too busy receiving emails. The phones would also not respond to being shut off manually.

My executive couldn't call me until he could get back to his laptop at his house, login and check for my number in Outlook because Splunk and the email notification system had effectively disabled control of his phone.

I assume it is embarrassing to have your cell phone buzzing non-stop during what's supposed to be a professional dinner to discuss operational efficiency (that was actually the topic).

The other fallout was that two other tier-3 systems (network and active directory) couldn't send any notifications because the email server was too busy and Splunk had filled up its email queue.

Now the moral of the story is simply this: Be very sure you need real-time alerting.

When Splunk says real time, it does mean real time, so helping your leadership understand the concept of time is very necessary before you break things that they didn't even know were in place.

Here are some things you might be able to try saying to your leadership that will help them with what they are asking for:

- Scheduling a real-time alert is very resource intensive for Splunk, so what if we try setting up an alert that runs every 5 minutes and checks 5 minutes of history?
- What if we schedule an alert for every 15 minutes and only send one alert in order to reduce the noise of the alerts we receive? (Insert monitoring system) is creating a lot of noisy alerts, which is something we are trying to get away from.
- What if we set up an alert to run every 1 minute to check 10 minutes of history? Then, if we receive an alert, we can throttle it to not send another alert for 30 minutes, and we can see how our team responds to know if we need to make adjustments to our processes.

There are millions of ways to avoid setting up real-time alerting and notifying on every result.

In order to avoid yelling, I suggest avoiding real-time alerting and notification unless absolutely necessary.

Here's the reality. It's very unlikely that any, and I do mean any, service team is going to react appropriately to sub-second alerting, and Splunk will send sub-second emails.

It's much easier to reach the goal of alerting **noise reduction** when we schedule an alert for human reaction time.

Depending on your service team, crafting an alert with the appropriate intelligence to trigger once in a 15 minute interval and then throttle notifications for 30 minutes is reasonable. That will give the people who are actually going to fix the problem a chance to resolve the problem before another alert triggers.

If your team has a better than 15 minute MTTR, then I congratulate you, as something like that in IT is similar to finding a unicorn for us humans. You may consider setting your thresholds differently.

To quickly summarize

If your boss asks for real-time alerting, don't assume he knows what he is asking for. They don't know that Splunk has the potential to cause bigger issues if you turn that on. Instead, try to determine what real time means to them. Does it mean an alert every minute, every ten minutes, or every sixty minutes?

In case you do end up in a situation where you need to turn on a real-time alert/notification, be sure to give ample warning to your superiors about what could happen if a machine spins out of control.

Be specific

Leadership has a way of delegating a task to Splunk admin and walking away. They don't realize that the task they just delegated may be like asking the Splunk admin to climb a beanstalk to find the golden goose after fighting the giant.

When I say "be specific" I mean be very specific about the system and data that is being displayed.

For instance, do not assume that the Splunk for Linux app will display all of the relevant charts for YOUR organization.

By this I mean the following.

If you have a very good engineering person in your organization that is well respected, you can expect them to have their own tools for monitoring.

You can also expect that they know the difference between using `vmstat` on Linux, and the same thing on Solaris and what it represents.

Vmstat on Solaris is probably one of the best commands to get data about memory from a Solaris machine, but any good Linux administrator knows that if you want info about memory from Red Hat or CentOS, you use free-g or top, or something of the sort, because `vmstat` doesn't accurately represent memory being used due to the cache.

It also just so happens that free-g doesn't exist on Solaris, and there really isn't an equivalent within the system tools packages available.

The `Splunk_TA_nix` only uses `vmstat` to gather memory information, so if you deploy that on your Linux machine and you see flat lines at the same value, then that will be why. Vmstat and free-m measure memory utilization differently on a Linux machine than on a Solaris machine.

Small details like this make all the difference in an alert being accurate and actionable, and being completely ignored by your service or ops team.

Vmstat is not the only instance of something like this within the NIX app, so before you launch ANY app, go through and be sure you're collecting the right data to alert on.

In order to present this question to your leadership, it simply requires a question like:

> *"Since you want to monitor Linux memory utilization, should we be using vmstat or free-m?"*

Allow them to decide and get back to you. If you decide, you will be held accountable for it not being what everyone expected when something goes wrong.

To quickly summarize

Be specific about the data you are alerting on, and make sure it is the data that the system owners agree is the most actionable data to alert on. If there are varying opinions, follow up with them about the decision that they need to make, and if time drags on, let leadership know what's going on. Things like which "counter" to use is very important for everyone to buy into for Splunk alerting to be accurate.

Predictions

With new technology comes new ideas and expectations. While some live in reality, others live in fantasy. Helping your leadership, as well as your team, understand the limitations of predictive analytics in Splunk will help you manage your workload.

It won't be too long after you start using predictive analytics and machine learning technology that a member of leadership will come to you to ask you how we can alert on it.

Make no mistake, this is a very slippery slope.

If it is part of your organization's roadmap to alert on the predictions made with Splunk, then I would suggest that you do these two things, and they are not guaranteed to save you if you come in wrong:

- Based on your time of prediction, have at least 3x the data points within your Splunk system.
    - This means that if you want to predict out 3 months use 9 months worth of data.
- Have Splunk predictions checked by a doctor of mathematics that understands the LLP algorithm. For more info, look on `http://www.splunk.com/` for the predict function.

It is often the case that people will ask you to predict things such as **capacity planning**, **bandwidth utilization**, or **market swing** using Splunk with no math expert to back you up.

To my fellow Splunkers, Splunkers holding accountability for one of the aforementioned things right now should be treated like a bomb that will explode if you tip it. Slowly set it down on the floor, stand up slowly while watching it, and walk away. When at a safe distance, run like the wind!

I exaggerate, but I would personally avoid predictive alerting altogether, unless there is a Ph.D involved, simply because of my experiences with it.

There is no biological or non-biological method known on earth that is capable of predicting the future. If there was one, I have no doubt everyone would know, and it would not be an enterprise software program.

If you have a mathematician with you to fact check for you, then knock yourself out. Splunk isn't a bad way to automate predicting functions, and it leverages big data clustering architecture for the increase of resource utilization quite well. It may make your calculations very quickly, depending on your architecture.

In order to avoid using predictive analytics to alert without a Ph.D, you can ask your leadership member questions/statements like:

- What if the data isn't right? I'm not a doctor in math, so I won't know, and then you will take that to your boss and it starts getting really bad if we're wrong.
- We need 3 years' worth of data to predict what it will look like next year and we don't have it.
- We need 10PB of SSD storage to hold 3 years' worth of capacity metrics. That will likely have a financial impact. Can we afford that kind of refresh?
- Splunk cannot tell the future, no matter what the sales guy said.

Things like this can help you to avoid predictive alerting.

To quickly summarize

It is best to avoid predictive alerting. If you have to use it, have someone well educated in math fact check Splunk's results and/or let your leadership know that you may not be alerting on what you'd hoped. Run a test that they would want, notifying only you and your leadership member to test this use case and see if Splunk is giving you the desired results before you publish them to other members of leadership.

Above are a lot of pages that seem to repeat the same message of **be careful what you alert on** at great length, repetitively, without ever getting to the how of the matter. You may wish to consider whether the preceding six pages could be capably reduced to four or five paragraphs.

Anatomy of an alert

There are some very fundamental parts of an alert that are generic to any alerting system. They are translatable to Nagios, SCOM, Icinga, or take your pick. In Splunk, however, there are some unique components of an alert that give us the ability to enhance what the alert itself does, and mostly it has to do with **SPL(Splunk Processing Language)**. Once we have gotten the results we want, there are some fun things we can do with an alert.

Search query results

This is the result set of any search that you determine viable for an alert. It is often easiest to use a stats command to set an alert, as it gives an integer that can easily be filtered by a where statement. The amount of history searched is also very important in the setup of an alert.

Alert naming

The naming convention you choose often doesn't sound very important at all. I can tell you that, usually, it is not, right up until you start collecting hundreds, if not thousands, of alerts, which does happen. Creating the appropriate naming convention eases administration, so, when you go looking to adjust an alert, you do not have to individually eyeball hundreds of alerts to find the one you are looking for. This is a huge time saver for the future.

The schedule

This will be the schedule that the alert itself runs on. This is set somewhere in time using either the Splunk default time choices or a Cron scheduler. The schedule is set to run this search every 5 minutes, or every hour, or every day. This will be the schedule that the alert runs this search on in order to potentially take action. This is also where people like to set "real-time" and break their systems. DO NOT set real-time alerts unless absolutely necessary. They are extremely taxing on your infrastructure.

The trigger

The trigger is the threshold that is set, which must be breached in order for an alert to take the next action within its programming. Consider the `if` statement of the function. `If count>0` then `<insert action>` kind of thing.

The action

This is the action taken by the system when triggered. This usually manifests itself in the form of an email to the appropriate stakeholders. However, in some instances this can also be running a script to restart a service or open a ticket. Some of the more advanced functions send tiered text messages, make phone calls with automated voice delivery systems, or follow escalation paths.

Throttling

This is a noise-reduction feature of Splunk that is actually quite nice. All throttling in Splunk is done by time, which usually translates like this: If an alert triggers, do not send another for `<insert time interval>`, even if the alert runs on its normally scheduled interval and finds another issue. The biggest pro for this feature is reducing the amount of noise coming from an alerting system.

Permissions

This is the last thing to set for an alert, which, while it may seem innocuous, if left unchecked, can become a certifiable nightmare. If you get in the good habit of setting permissions appropriately when you build your alert, it will help you should you ever have to migrate them to another search head or another app in the future.

Location of action scripts

Perhaps one more here. In case you intend to use an action, you need to consider where that action script should reside and whether the search head can (with requisite permissions) reach that location and trigger it. A particularly important consideration for Splunk Cloud users.

Example

Let's use an example, so we can build an alert here that is often asked for in the real world. We're going to make a basic CPU alert for our Linux machines.

Our leadership has stated that they want the service team to receive an alert when the CPU utilization on any machine reaches more than 90% for a sustained period of time. In our case, the sustained period is 15 minutes. They don't want to see this alert more than one time every half an hour.

To do this, we must first create the search itself to display the data.

Using the `Splunk_TA_nix` app to gather the information, its default sourcetypes and field extractions, we can calculate the CPU load using some of the fields it provides.

Here is the search we will be using:

```
index=nix sourcetype=cpucpu=all | evalpctCPU=(100 - pctIdle) | stats
avg(pctCPU) as cpu by host
```

This search result set looks like this:

You may be asking why I added the calculation within this search when the data itself says `pctCPU`. Why are you calculating it again when it's already doing it for you?

The reason for this, in Linux, is quite simple. It's because there are multiple fields within the `sar -P 1 1` command (which is how Splunk is getting this data) that represent different aspects of CPU utilization, none of which give a full picture in a single field. The script itself is doing some calculations. However, it is a long-understood caveat in the script that collects CPU data for Splunk that states that the data is accurate for each field, but if you want actual machine load, it will need to be calculated within Splunk.

To get full machine load, we need to use the percent idle field. You may ask "why?" Because, no matter what CPU function is being utilized, it will always take away from the idle process. If we use the simple formula (`100- pctIdle`), we are creating the full CPU load of a machine for each event over the entire machine in Linux.

The next question we need to understand is: Exactly what does this result set represent?

These results have been gotten by using the above search over a 15 minute period, which means we are receiving the average of the all values within the `sar` command over 15 minutes.

While that's helpful, the next step is to only see machines with values of this average above 90%, so we need to add a filter to our search:

```
index=nix sourcetype=cpucpu=all | evalpctCPU=(100 - pctIdle) | stats
avg(pctCPU) as cpu by host | where cpu>90
```

At the time of running this search, I didn't have any machines that were over 90%, so I had to use CPU>25, but you should get the idea:

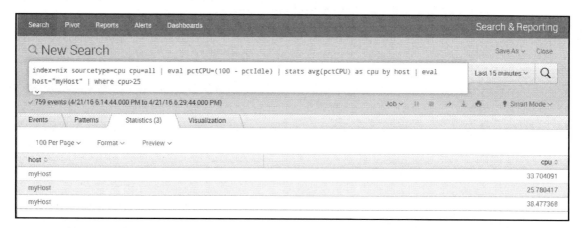

Now that we have filtered out all of the machines that have a 15-minute average CPU utilization that's more than 90%, how can we have Splunk tell us about a sustained behavior?

The magic is still within the search syntax. First, we have to create a few categories for us to begin bucketing our results into, which we can use to filter. In this case, I like to use severity, as it is easy to set those thresholds.

We can do this with an `eval` statement in our search query:

```
index=nix sourcetype=cpucpu=all startminutesago=30
| evalpctCPU=(100 - pctIdle)
| eval severity=case(pctCPU>=90, "Critical", pctCPU>=70, "Warning",
pctCPU>=0, "Normal")
| where severity="Critical"
| stats avg(pctCPU) as cpu count by host severity
```

This will then give categories to each instance in our result set that will help us, and it will also provide some more information in the alert when triggered:

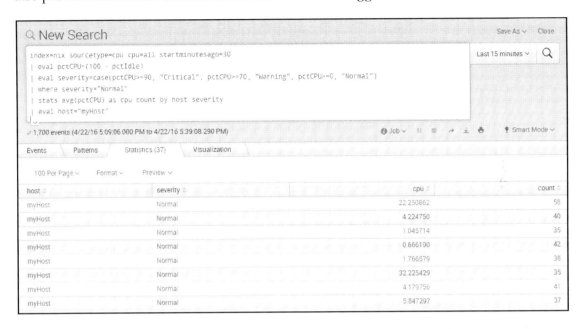

Again, from my example, you can see that my filter is set to look for anything greater than or equal to 25, which should be set to 90. I simply didn't have the results in my system at the time of writing this.

When we add this `eval` statement, our severity category appears for our results and we can then perform our stats function, which will give us the averages we are looking for.

Now that we have the 30-minute average, how do we find the sustained behavior of our CPU that our leadership has asked for?

We leverage our time intervals and count them.

In the `inputs.conf` of your `Splunk_TA_nix` on your Linux forwarders, there is going to be a section for this data input that is set to a time interval.

That will look something like this:

```
# Shows stats per CPU (useful for SMP machines)
[script://./bin/cpu.sh]
sourcetype = cpu
source = cpu
interval = 30
index = nix
disabled = 0
```

In this case, we care the most about the **interval** setting. We can see that, above, it is set for 30-second polling intervals. That being known, we can figure out how many 30-second intervals there are in a 30-minute period, and then use that number to filter by.

There are 60 of these intervals within a 30-minute period, so if we wanted a sustained interval of 15 minutes, then we would need to filter by our count of 30.

That part of the search looks like this:

```
index=nix sourcetype=cpucpu=all startminutesago=30
| evalpctCPU=(100 - pctIdle)
| eval severity=case(pctCPU>=90, "Critical", pctCPU>=70, "Warning",
pctCPU>=0, "Normal")
| where severity="Critical"
| stats avg(pctCPU) as cpu count by host severity
| where count>30
```

This gives us some results that look like this:

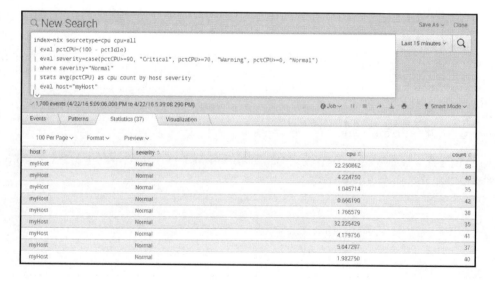

This search is now showing us only the results that have a sustained category of critical for more than 15 minutes. The next step is simply formatting the result set to look nice in an alert.

We just need to sort it, add a % symbol, and remove any extra fields we used during development.

The final search query looks like this:

```
index=nix sourcetype=cpucpu=all
| evalpctCPU=(100 - pctIdle)
| eval severity=case(pctCPU>=90, "Critical", pctCPU>=70, "Warning",
pctCPU>=0, "Normal")
| where severity="Normal"
| stats avg(pctCPU) as cpu count by host severity
| eval host="myHost"
| where count>30
| evalcpu=round(cpu,1)
| sort - cpu
| evalcpu=(cpu + "%")
| fields - count
```

This has an output that looks like this:

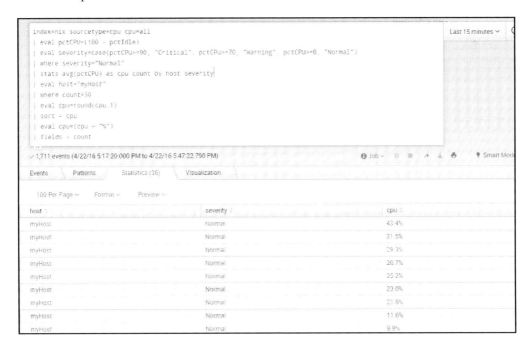

This result set is ultimately what your alert will be sending to your email recipients, which is just what our leadership asked for. The next steps are quite easy. We simply save the alert using our decided naming convention, and set our schedule, trigger condition, action, and throttling.

The historical data is important to remember here because we need to set this search to look back over at least 30 minutes of data for the alert that we have made to be effective.

Using SPL we can set our earliest and latest times, and then, to set our schedule of 30 minutes (since it's not a default), we just write a Cron expression.

Our trigger condition will be set to trigger if we get even a single result. However, if multiple results occur, Splunk will bundle them into the same alert to reduce noise:

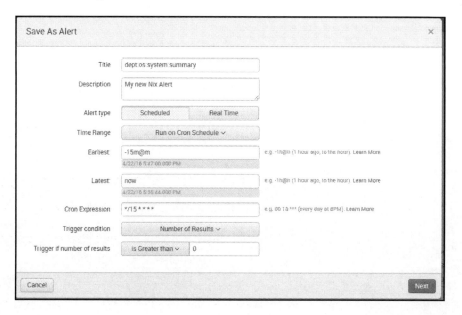

Now, after our alert name, historical dataset, and trigger condition have been chosen, we can determine which actions Splunk will take.

In this case, we will set Splunk to email a distribution company (make sure your SH is setup for SMTP!) with the search results. In this case, we will throttle our alert by 30 minutes:

Once we click on **Save**, our alert will be active, and we just need to communicate success to our leadership.

By the way, these last few pages were excellent. Clear, and easy to follow. Nice. Perhaps the six pages of warnings about poorly configured alerts could be replaced with a few well-positioned sentences among the description of steps in the alert process?

Custom commands/automated self-healing

Using **custom commands** is an advanced feature within Splunk, and requires a Python developer in order to create one. The advantage to this is that, if you have a system that you need to run a command on in real time to, say, check memory utilization, CPU utilization, or even unlock a user account or restart a service, you can leverage this technique and then have your Splunk alerts/searches perform these functions in real time. It really might be a good idea to reference the free, pre-built alert action apps on Splunkbase. They can be an extremely valuable jumping-off point for someone who wants to build a custom action, but perhaps isn't sure how to. Let's say we want to restart a remote service when a specific log message occurs more than 30 times because that means the application itself has hit a wall and is no longer functioning.

Let me add that this is not a good thing to do. The ideal situation is to leverage your internal process to get development to investigate what is occurring and why the application is crashing. In the meantime, however, this can be an option.

Let's also say we've already written our Python script to restart services, it lives in the default location of `/opt/splunk/myApp/bin/remote.py`, and that it looks like this:

```python
import sys
import splunk.Intersplunk
import subprocess
import logging
import os

# System logging
logger = logging.getLogger('testssh')
hdlr = logging.FileHandler('/tmp/testssh.txt')
formatter = logging.Formatter('%(asctime)s %(levelname)s %(message)s')
hdlr.setFormatter(formatter)
logger.addHandler(hdlr)
logger.setLevel(logging.INFO)

try:

keywords,options = splunk.Intersplunk.getKeywordsAndOptions() # Get all the
options passed

    # Check for passed parameters
    if not options.has_key('host'):
splunk.Intersplunk.generateErrorResults("no host specified")
        exit(0)
    if not options.has_key('user'):
splunk.Intersplunk.generateErrorResults("no user specified")
        exit(0)
```

```
    if not options.has_key('command'):
splunk.Intersplunk.generateErrorResults("no pids specified")
        exit(0)

    command = options.get('command', None)
    host = options.get('host', None)
    user = options.get('user', None)

results,dummy,settings = splunk.Intersplunk.getOrganizedResults()
    for r in results:
        try:
            # Call the script passing all the necessary arguments
            p = subprocess.Popen(["ssh","-i","/ /home/user1/.ssh/id_rsa","-
q","-t","-t",r[user]+"@"+r[host],r[command]],stdin=subprocess.PIPE,
stdout=subprocess.PIPE,stderr=subprocess.STDOUT)
            # Get the output from script and push it to new output column
out,err = p.communicate()
            #logger.info(out.decode("utf-8"))
            r["output"]= out.decode("utf-8")
            r["error"]=err
            r["return_code"]=p.returncode;
        except ValueError, e:
            results = splunk.Intersplunk.generateErrorResults(str(e))
        except OSError, e:
            results = splunk.Intersplunk.generateErrorResults(str(e))

    #Output results back to Splunk
splunk.Intersplunk.outputResults(results)

except Exception, e:
    results = splunk.Intersplunk.generateErrorResults(str(e))
```

This script will perform any standard Linux command on any remote system as long as the user you have written into this script has permissions to commit that action. If your results that print are anything other than '0' then it didn't work.

Also, make sure to have the user in your script have passwordless login rights on your destination machine, so copy those SSH keys.

So, since the script exists in /opt/splunk/etc/apps/myApp/bin on my search head, I now need to actually add the command itself so I can let the Splunk search head know that it is there.

To do this, we edit `commands.conf` in our app
(`/opt/splunk/etc/apps/myApp/local/commands.conf`).

In that file, we add the following settings:

```
[remote_call]
filename = remote.py
streaming = true
```

Then we restart our search head. When we do, the command will then be active, and to run it we need only add the | `remote_call<field1><field2><field3>` at the end of our search to invoke the call. In this case, those fields are `hostpid` and `command`.

Here is the search query that invokes this external operation:

```
eventtype=myService_failure
| stats eventcount by host user command pid
| eval command="/usr/local/bin/sudokill ".pid
| where count<30
| sort - count
| remote_call host=host user=user command=command
```

Here we are setting the command `/usr/local/bin/sudo kill <pid#>` to run on any host that populates in the result set with more than 30 of our saved events occurring. Now we can set this as an alert over 15 minutes and then throttle it for 60 minutes, and we will have an automated operation of service restarts based on application log events.

This has been called self-healing or automation.

A word of warning

When you setup automated functions like this, be very careful. It is very easy to have something like this spin out of control. What do I mean by that?

Let's use the example above.

Let's say we are running our alert on a 5-minute schedule, we are searching back through 60 minutes' worth of data, and we automate our alert to restart a service after 30 messages like before.

When that log has written 60 messages, our alert is going to trigger, then it will trigger again in 5 minutes, and then again in another 5 minutes, and so on because we are searching 60 minutes' worth of data.

Basically, those events will have to roll out of our 60-minute window, and, until they do, the service will be restarting every 5 minutes.

This is only a single scenario where this can be bad. There are so many others, so if you are going to try this technique, be sure to use a test system or something that is very low impact to work out any kinks. Splunk will not support you in this venture either, so you are on your own with this one.

Summary

In this chapter, we have discussed the growing importance of Splunk alerting and the different levels of doing so. In the current corporate environment, intelligent alerting and alert noise reduction are becoming more important due to machine sprawl, both horizontally and vertically. Then we discussed how to create intelligent alerts and manage them effectively, and also some methods of self-healing that I've used in the past, and the successes and consequences of such methods in order to assist in setting expectations. In the next chapter, we will talk about the anatomy of a search and then some key techniques that will help in real world scenarios. Many people understand search syntax. However, to use it effectively, (that is, to become a search ninja) is something much more evasive and continuous. I will use real-world use-cases in order to get the point across, such as merging two datasets at search time, and making the result set of two searches match each other in time.

6
Searching and Reporting

We are going to learn about the *not-so-common* searching and reporting techniques that have been used in real-world scenarios in order to present data both accurately and in the pretty format that leadership asks us for. There are also some caveats to the **Search Processing Language** that we need to understand when performing a search, not only for presentation purposes, but also for presenting accurate data.

We will learn about:

- General practices (efficiencies):
    - Core fields
    - Case sensitivity
    - Inclusive versus exclusive
- Search modes:
    - Fast Mode
    - Smart Mode
    - Verbose Mode
- Advanced charting:
    - Overlay
    - Xyseries
    - Appending results
    - Day-over-day overlay

General practices

Of course we can search whatever we want in Splunk, using it in a similar way to the way we use Google, for our log files, but there are some ways to make searching itself more efficient, and faster. There are a few things to understand when making your query practice more efficient, and I will use a few that are commonly overlooked.

This may be more editorial than technical, but it might be helpful here, to quickly describe the three components of a Splunk search before starting to explain core search. This seems to help a lot of people to understand searching as a concept:

- Core search (what data will be included in the search?):
- Function or calculation
- Formatting or presentation

Let's see an example of them:

1. Perform a Core search:

   ```
   Index=test index sourcetype=bookstuff action=purchase
   ```

2. Then add a function or calculation:

   ```
   Index=test index sourcetype=bookstuff action=purchase |
   stats avg(latency) as Delay by host
   ```

3. Then tell Splunk how to present the results:

   ```
   Index=test index sourcetype=bookstuff action=purchase |
   stats avg(latency) as Delay by host | table host Delay
   ```

Now that layout is clear, it might be easier to explain each component in more depth.

Core fields (root search)

There are a few fields that Splunk writes to disk by default, and they can go quite far in helping you decrease search times. Using as many as these fields as you can as part of your root search will help you decrease your query time.

_time

Time is always the most effective filter when performing searches. If you can limit the time you are searching, you limit the amount of data that Splunk has to look through, in order to find your results.

Index

Pointing Splunk to a specific index at the time of search begins filtering the data out that you don't want to see. The `index` field will relegate the rest of the query to that dataset (not including subsearches and joins, and so on) and will assist in bringing down the search time considerably.

Sourcetype

The `sourcetype` field is a way to limit the amount of data searched to a specific subset of the whole. Often when inputting data into Splunk, each log type is a different dataset which is allocated as a separate `sourcetype` such as IIS, **firewall**, or **syslog** in order to define the dataset.

Host

The `host` field is written to disk at indexing time and also limits the amount of data that Splunk has to search through in order to get you the results you're looking for. If you have 500 machines dumping data to Splunk, and you only care about four hosts for your specific search, just use the `OR` clause to search those hosts.

Source

The `source` field is often the actual filepath/logfile that is being ingested, and if you can use this field then it also helps to reduce the amount of time your searches take. Often using the `source` field is not practical; however you can use it in your query and if it makes sense, it will help your search return results faster as well.

The moral of using these fields is that the more specific you can be with Splunk, the faster it will return the results, and specifically the results you want to see. With Splunk, the devil is in the detail, and the details in Splunk are so granular that we have to train our eyes to look for the smallest things that could affect our results. It can be as simple as a capital *T* where it should be lowercase *t*. A single character can throw off your result set by an amazing amount, so the more info you can give Splunk the better.

As a best practice, if you use only the fields you care about after your root search, you will increase your search times as well.

Take for instance `iis` data:

If this is your original search:

```
index=access_combined sourcetype=iis
```

And you wanted to increase your search times, you could add only the fields you care about like this:

```
index=access_combined sourcetype=iis | fields host cs_host time_taken cs_ip
sc_ip User
```

And you should see improvements in the returned results .

Case sensitivity

Case sensitivity doesn't matter too much in Splunk, but it does make a difference when searching in order not to get **No results found**. Case sensitivity is generally understood in SPL, but I've only seen it written down in a few places, so I figured I would present those to you here.

Here is a table that should explain most of what is case sensitive, and what's not:

Case Sensitive	Example
Boolean operators	AND, OR, NOT
Field names	ipAddr **versus** ipaddr
Lookup field values	vendorName=Verizon **versus** vendorName=verizon
Regular expressions	\d\d\d **versus** \D\D\D

if and case functions (eval/where commands)	`eval action=if(action=="login",...)`
	`where action="login"`
	`stats count(eval(action="login") as...`

CASE()	CASE(login)
Tags	infosec **versus** INFOSEC

Inclusive versus exclusive

On that note as well, inclusive searches are generally better than exclusive searches. Meaning that using terms to include data you want is going to be faster than attempting to exclude data you don't want to see. Sometimes it's unavoidable, although, in my mind, knowing this kind of information is often better than not knowing. It may also be important to note the AND function of Splunk is implied here, so `host=host1 AND host=host2` is not necessary.

As an example:

```
index=access_combined sourcetype=iis host!=host1 host!=host5 | fields host
cs_host time_taken cs_ip sc_ip User
```

Will generally be slower at returning results than:

```
index=access_combined sourcetype=iis host=host2 OR host=host2 OR host=host3
| fields host cs_host time_taken cs_ip sc_ip User
```

Search modes

For the more advanced Splunker, search modes are quite important, and can save you plenty of time when speaking with a user that isn't very Splunk savvy. I will simply recap these, and mention that by default, Splunk runs in **Smart Mode**.

If you would like to change the mode in a search, just use the mode selector drop-down menu, below the time range picker, after you run a query.

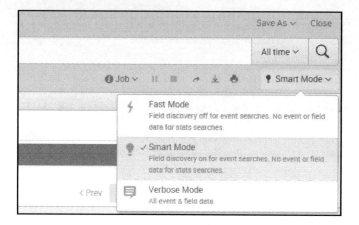

Fast Mode

Fast Mode in Splunk will search all of the data you ask for, and then only return the essential parts of that data in its result set, as well as the fields you mentioned in your query. This will omit any unused fields, and no event data. So basically you will have `sourcetype`, `source`, `host`, and whatever fields you ask for from your data in your result set and that is all.

 Note that **Field Discovery** is **off** on **Fast Mode**, which is why it will only return the fields you ask for.

Here is an example of running a fast search:

```
index=network sourcetype=fw | stats count by service | sort - count | head
10
```

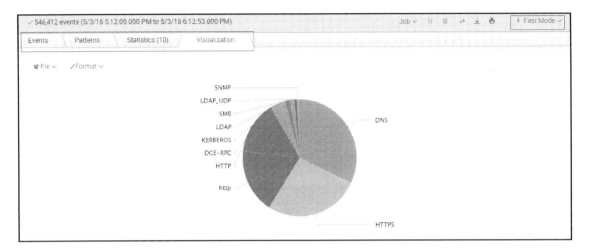

When we go to the job inspector we can see how long this job actually took:

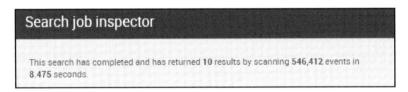

Verbose Mode

Verbose Mode is usually the slowest of the searching modes, though it also produces the most information to look through. In **Verbose Mode**, **Field Discovery** is **on**, and you will also see all event data within the time frame you are searching.

Notice the **Events** tab is now populated with data.

Here is an example of searching in **Verbose Mode**:

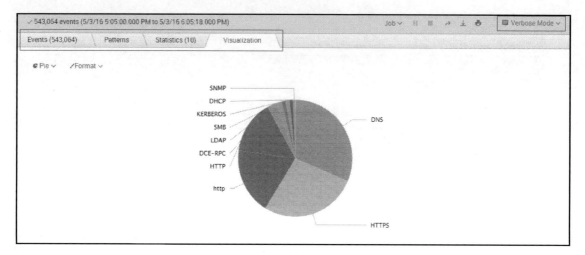

When we go to the job inspector we can see how long this job actually took:

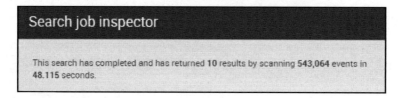

Smart Mode (default)

Smart Mode is a combination of Fast and Verbose Mode searching. **Field Discovery** is **on**, like in **Verbose Mode**, though depending on how much you put in your query, you may or may not get event data. In short, if you have a transformative section in your search, say like a `stats` or `timechart` function, you won't get any event data. If you use only the root search however, you will see events populate just like in Verbose Mode.

Here is an example of searching the same data in **Smart Mode**:

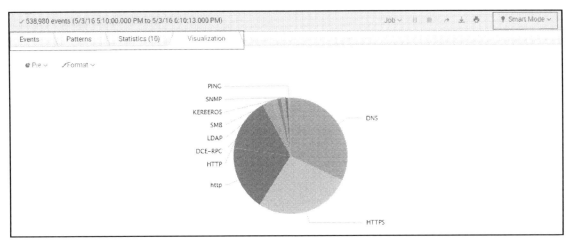

When we go to the job inspector we can see how long this job actually took:

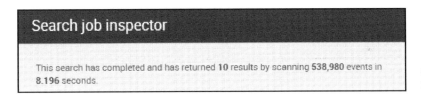

Now you'll notice that this is a touch faster than **Fast Mode**, and in this case I will assume that it's because I was searching real time, and the timeframe I set was moving. Notice the number of events in **Fast Mode** versus this search.

Advanced charting

Charting in itself is one of the most helpful tools to visualize data; however, there are some things that leadership may ask for that are more difficult, and may come down to something as simple as reformatting a chart to switch the X and Y axis, or overlaying results week over week to show change. There are some common techniques that you can use to get the job done, which we will discuss here.

Overlay

Making charts is great; however, sometimes the boss wants everything in a single pane. There are lots of different ways we can make a chart overlay with our data, but here we are only going to discuss a single use case.

In this overlay, we are only going to discuss how to perform these functions using a single axis as your point of overlay.

Host CPU / MEM utilization

Let's say that our Linux engineering team would like a way to be able to view the CPU and MEM utilization of a single host, and search it through time. They would like to build a dashboard with this panel in it at some point, so that they won't have to remember the search, and so they can make this part of their daily checks / troubleshooting tasks.

Knowing that we already have the `Splunk_TA_nix` (Linux add on) installed appropriately across our Linux environment and we have confirmed that data is flowing into Splunk as expected, we will then need to build our search one source type at a time.

First let's get our CPU metrics straight. To do that we need to point our root search query at the Linux CPU data, and a specific host. Remember to start with a small time period, say 15 minutes, until the query has matured:

```
index=nix sourcetype=cpu cpu=all host=myHost1
```

Now that we have the CPU portion, let's find the memory data:

```
index=nix sourcetype=freeMem host=myHost
```

Now we just need to join the two datasets in a single query:

```
index=nix (sourcetype=cpu cpu=all host=myHost OR (sourcetype=freeMem
host=myHost
```

That should look something like this:

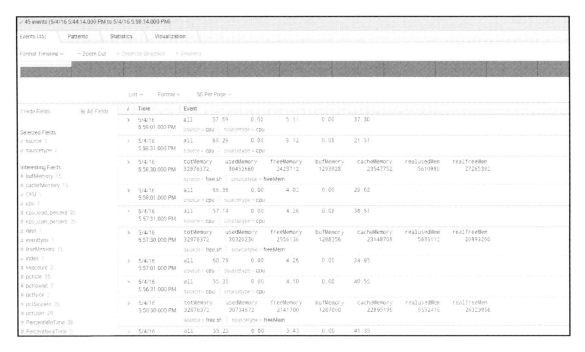

You'll notice the combined datasets, and all of the fields relevant to both sourcetypes within this image. That's exactly what we're looking for.

Next we need to do some calculation, in order to turn the **cpu** and memory into a simple 0-100% scale that our leadership would like to see.

To do that we just add a few `eval` statements, and then present the data to a timechart:

```
index=nix (sourcetype=cpu cpu=all host=myHost OR (sourcetype=freeMem
host=myHost | eval cpu=(100 - pctIdle) | eval mem=((realusedMem /
totMemory) * 100) | timechart avg(cpu) as cpu, avg(mem) as mem
```

Which will look something like this on a 15-minute line chart:

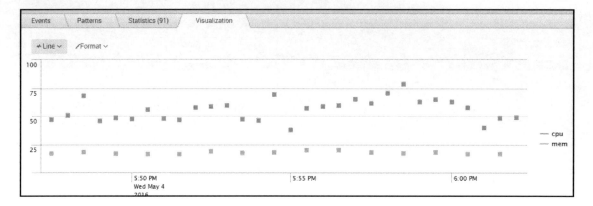

Now that we have the combined data in a timechart, the rest is just formatting, and extending the time range.

So now, let's first extend the time to 60 minutes to make Splunk connect the dots, turn this chart into an area chart, and then we can add our overlay by going to **Format** | **Overlay**.

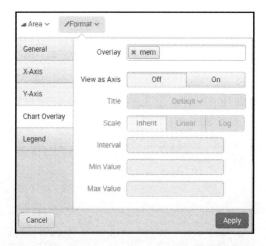

When we add one of our fields (in this case I chose **mem**) to the **Overlay** field, and click apply, we will get our happily formatted overlay of MEM over CPU for our engineering staff.

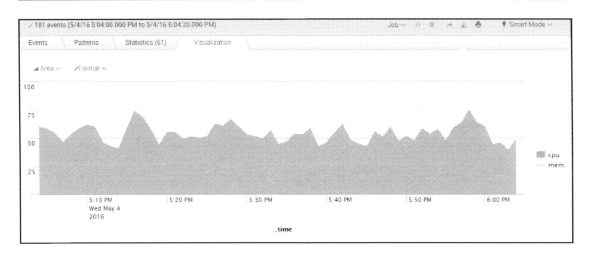

Xyseries

Xyseries is a command that is very similar to the timechart command, except it's more versatile in the way that you can format your visualization. With the `timechart` command, you will always be relegated to using **_time** as your *X* axis, because whatever you're charting, it must be *over* time with the possibility of using a split-by clause. With xyseries, you have the ability to remove **_time** from your chart, and report on other interesting things in your data.

One of the advantages is that you can use xyseries to reformat data after a stats statement and a filter. There are a few things to note in the format of the xyseries command.

```
Xyseries <field1> <field2> <field3>
```

- `field1`: The field to become the x-axis
- `field2`: The field that has the values that will be used as labels
- `field3`: The field that has the data that's going to be charted

Here is an example of searching transaction types over an international organization, and which department they belong to.

If we get a query that leverages the `chart` function like this one:

```
index=bi_data sourcetype=transact action=commit | chart count by catdesc dstcountry
```

We may get an output that looks like this:

catdesc	Belgium	Canada	Chile	Germany	Ireland	OTHER	Reserved	Singapore	Sweden	United Kingdom	United States
Advertising	0	7	16	0	49	2	17	0	0	0	1322
Armed Forces	0	0	0	0	0	0	0	0	0	0	9
Arts and Culture	0	0	0	0	0	0	0	0	0	0	7
Business	0	3	0	0	6	1	0	0	0	0	120
Content Servers	0	3	0	0	2	0	0	0	0	0	89
Domain Parking	0	0	0	0	0	0	0	0	0	0	1
Education	0	0	0	0	0	0	0	0	0	0	12
Entertainment	0	0	0	0	0	0	0	0	0	0	23
Finance and Banking	0	0	0	0	0	0	0	0	0	0	67
Folklore	0	0	0	0	0	0	0	0	0	0	1

This shows us the data we are looking for; however, we may want to filter that down from expected behavior. Let's say we expect an average of 10 transactions for each of these categories.

When we try to add a `where count > 10` filter to our query with the `chart` function, we will get **No results found**:

```
index=bi_data sourcetype=transact action=commit | chart count by catdesc
dstcountry | where count > 10
```

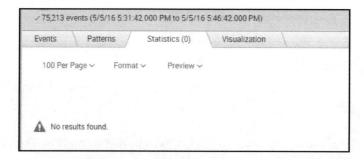

In this case, because all we want to do is filter the data a bit, we can use the `stats` command with the `xyseries` function:

```
index=bi_data sourcetype=transact action=commit
| stats count by catdesc dstcountry
| where count > 10
| xyseries catdesc dstcounrty count
```

```
| fillnull value="-"
```

This will give us a nice table with our filtered data in it:

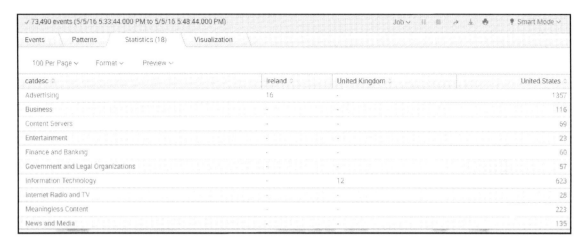

catdesc	Ireland	United Kingdom	United States
Advertising	16	-	1357
Business	-	-	116
Content Servers	-	-	69
Entertainment	-	-	23
Finance and Banking	-	-	60
Government and Legal Organizations	-	-	57
Information Technology	-	12	623
Internet Radio and TV	-	-	28
Meaningless Content	-	-	223
News and Media	-	-	135

Appending results

Appending results in a chart is a bit of a tricky process, but can come in handy for correlating data within a visualization. Whether you are using a timechart, or the stats command, there is a small piece to the end of your query that will save you hours of headache and make your data accurate.

timechart

When we append data within a timechart, Splunk doesn't "make it look like we want". I put that in quotes because that's what most leadership will say when they see this for the first time. This is another example of proper formatting to please leadership; however, the data isn't wrong, and neither is Splunk.

As an example, let's take the same data that we used in the xyseries example, which is the transactions of an international organization. In this example, we won't care about the type of transactions, we will simply be counting how many there are over time by country. Let's say we want to compare two in the same chart.

We want to compare the United States and Ireland, and see how many transactions occurred through time by each country.

To do this we will first need to get the data for a single country. Let's start with the United States.

```
index=bi_data sourcetype=transact action=commit dstcounrty="United States"
| timechart count by dstcountry
```

This will give us the first line of our chart:

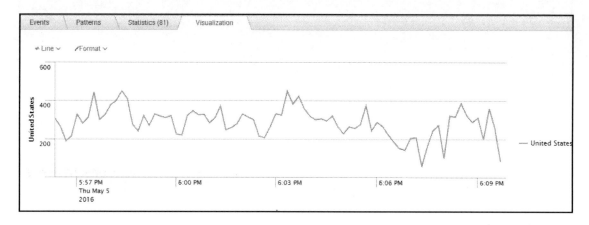

Then we will need to use the `append` command to add the rest of our data, but when we do so, Splunk literally appends the data to the end of the search. This messes up the chart's visualization if we don't do it right.

Our search with the append command would look like this:

```
index=bi_data sourcetype=transact action=commit dstcountry="United States"
| timechart count by dstcountry
| append [search index=bi_data sourcetype=transact action=commit
dstcountry="Ireland"
| timechart count by dstcountry]
```

This will give us a chart that is elongated, and not very useful:

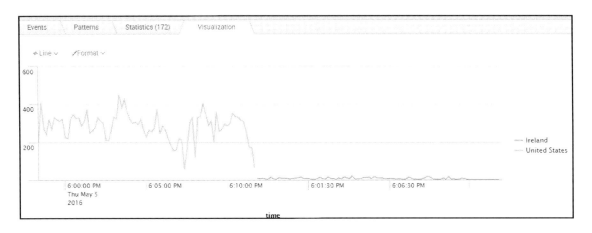

If you were to show leadership this chart, you would get a reaction that could be summed up by saying "go back and fix it to make it what I wanted".

You will see that the countries and the times don't line up because the `append` command is not supposed to care about time, it simply appends the subsearch results to the end of the primary search.

To adjust this, we need to use another `timechart` command, to make sure the data lines up.

Our final query looks like this:

```
index=bi_data sourcetype=transact action=commit dstcountry="United States"
| timechart count by dstcountry
| append [search index=bi_data sourcetype=transact action=commit
dstcountry="Ireland"
| timechart count by dstcountry]
| timechart first(*) as *
```

This gives us an image of one country over another through time:

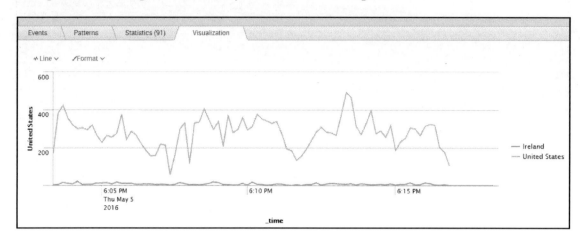

Always remember to use the `first (*) as *` function when combining/overlaying datasets.

stats

When using the `stats` command to count things, and then append more data to your table, it's sometimes hard to keep the data straight. It's better to use the `append` command rather than the `appendcols` command due to accuracy.

We will be using the same data as we used previously for this example as well.

This is a search using `append`, and our `first (*) by *` command to align the data. We will use the following query to retrieve how many transactions there were by country in the last hour, and then in the last 15 minutes:

```
index=bi_data sourcetype=transact action=commit earliest=-1h@h latest=@h
| stats count as "Last Hour" by dstcountry
| append [search index=bi_data sourcetype=transact action=commit
earliest=-15m@m latest=@m
| stats count as "Last 15 Minutes" by dstcountry]
| stats first(*) as * by dstcountry
| table dstcountry "Last Hour" "Last 15 Minutes"
```

dstcountry	Last Hour	Last 15 Minutes
Australia	35	1
Austria	1	
Belgium	1	
Brazil	3	1
Canada	308	66
Chile	56	
China	23	1
Costa Rica	6	
Denmark	3	
Europe	20	4
France	30	1
Germany	68	23
Greece	1	
Hong Kong	10	1
India	11	2
Ireland	2610	739
Italy	1	
Japan	111	58
Lithuania	3	
Luxembourg	2	
Netherlands	95	11
Norway	4	
Poland	3	2
Reserved	237557	53087
Russian Federation	5	1
Singapore	193	33
Sweden	52	7
Switzerland	11	6
Taiwan	1	
United Kingdom	405	63
United States	117517	24083

Notice where the blank spots are, and how the data lines up.

Now if we are to use the `appendcols` function of the `stats` command, we will get the same data but it will look different, as Splunk is appending the column itself, and not lining up the results to match.

Here is our query:

```
index=bi_data sourcetype=transact action=commit earliest=-1h@h latest=@h
| stats count as "Last Hour" by dstcountry
| appendcols [search index=bi_data sourcetype=transact action=commit
earliest=-15m@m latest=@m
| stats count as "Last 15 Minutes" by dstcountry]
```

And our result set looks a bit different.

The Week-over-Week-overlay

dstcountry ⇕	Last Hour ⇕	Last 15 Minutes ⇕
Austria	1	1
Belgium	1	57
Brazil	3	1
Canada	308	2
Chile	56	3
China	23	9
Costa Rica	6	1
Denmark	3	2
Europe	20	621
France	30	1
Germany	68	72
Greece	1	1
Hong Kong	10	6
India	11	2
Ireland	2610	55371
Italy	1	2
Japan	111	21
Lithuania	3	6
Luxembourg	2	9
Netherlands	95	76
Norway	4	23135
Poland	3	
Reserved	237557	
Russian Federation	5	
Singapore	193	
Sweden	52	
Switzerland	11	
Taiwan	1	
United Kingdom	405	
United States	117517	

Notice where the blank spaces are now, and how Splunk is appending the results set.

This is how we can give bad data to our leadership if we aren't careful.

Day-over-day overlay

Making historical overlays is something that can always benefit a current troubleshooting endeavor, as we can take a look at what happened yesterday compared to today, or last week compared to this week. To do this in Splunk, there are a couple of ways, and as with anything, there is the easy way, and the hard way. The easy way is to use the Timewrap app from Splunk, and the hard way is to use SPL (the query language) to do this.

SPL to overlay (the hard way)

Using SPL to do this can be a bit tricky, but for this we will use an example with the preceding dataset, so that we can keep this contiguous with the techniques we've learned so far.

Let's say our leadership wanted to understand how many transactions were made as a total over the past couple of days. They want to see yesterday's total transactions versus today's transactions. (This method can be used with weeks or months as well.)

In this case, our query will be using a subsearch to get this data, as well as the `appendcols` command in order to append our data appropriately.

Here is our query:

```
index=bi_data sourcetype=transact action=commit earliest=-24h@h latest=@h
| timechart span=1h count as "Transactions Today"
| appendcols [search index=bi_data sourcetype=transact action=commit
earliest=-48h@h latest=-24h@h
| timechart span=1h count as "Transactions Yesterday"]
| rename _time as hour
| eval hour=strftime(hour, "%H")
```

This will give us a chart that overlays yesterday over today by hourly buckets:

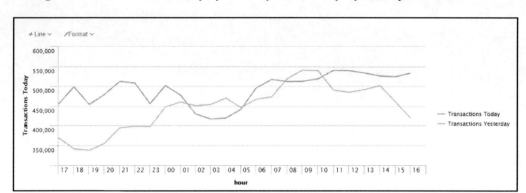

If you would like to do weeks, and change the formatting, just change your earliest/latest times, and then your `strftime eval` statement to match what you would like.

Timewrap (the easy way)

This is an app that was developed by a great person who decided that SPL was very painful to do time overlays with. This being true in the earlier versions of Splunk, a user built a Python script to help us out. That Python script was built into a Splunk command that works beautifully. I suggest installing this app, and making its perms global so you can at least test its functionality. Here is the link:

```
https://splunkbase.splunk.com/app/1645/
```

Install this, and follow the documentation on how to use it.

Summary

In this chapter, you have learnt about the anatomy of a search, and then some key techniques that help in real-world scenarios. Many people understand search syntax; however, to use it effectively (in other words, to become a search ninja) is something much more evasive and continuous. We have also seen real-world use cases in order to get the point across such as merging two datasets at search time, and making the result set of two searches match each other in time.

In the next chapter, I will show the readers how to create form-based dashboards leveraging `$foo$` variables as selectors to appropriately pass information to another search, or another dashboard, effectively creating a **drill-down** effect.

7
Form-Based Dashboards

In this chapter, we will discuss how to create some drilldown dashboards, and add some fun functionality such as contextual drilldowns and passing variables from form to form. Form-based dashboards ease the Splunk adoption process and enable a developer to build apps that a user can simply point and click, and report on the information that they need. This helps less knowledgeable users get value out of the data that is being consumed by Splunk.

We will learn about:

- Reports
- Dashboards
    - Form-based
    - Search-based
    - Drilldown
    - Report/Data model
- Modules
    - Data input
    - Chart
    - Table
    - Single value
    - Map module
- Tokens
- Building a form-based dashboard

Dashboards versus reports

The differences in dashboards and reports is pretty slight, although important to note, because in Splunk you can do different things with each of these, and in some cases you can build dashboards with reports that enhance the performance of your dashboard.

Reports

Reports are basically saved searches that you can access by clicking a link. They can be referenced by dashboards in order to create specific panels, and you can accelerate their performance with Splunk's **acceleration** option. You cannot accelerate a dashboard without leveraging a report or a data model of some sort. Reports are individual searches that populate results into a single panel.

I'll start by using one of the most common report examples for an operations infrastructure team, the disk space utilization report. I'm going to use Linux-based systems for my example. This example will assume that you have the **Splunk_TA_nix** add-on installed across your entire Linux environment.

Finding the information we are looking for is as simple as looking at our common command outputs for df. In Splunk, the root search starts with this data:

```
index=os sourcetype=df
```

This in turn gives us the events of our df output:

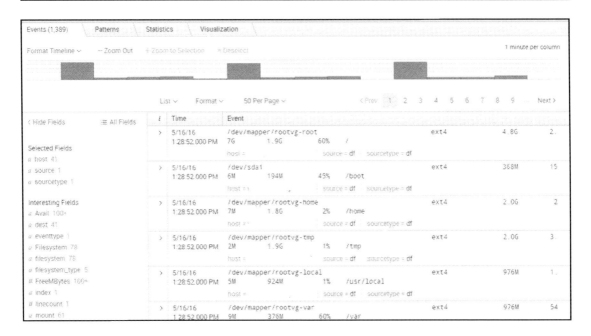

If our deployment was successful at the search tier, indexing tier, and forwarding tier, the fields that we will need to use for this example will be auto-extracted.

Here we will be averaging the used space by mount on every mount within our environment, and which host they live on:

```
index=nix sourcetype=df
| stats avg(PercentUsedSpace) AS pctSpace by mount host
| eval pctSpace=round(pctSpace)
```

And then we will add a filter to it, to create relevance to people:

```
index=nix sourcetype=df
| stats avg(PercentUsedSpace) AS pctSpace by mount host
| eval pctSpace=round(pctSpace)
| where pctSpace > 90
| sort - pctSpace
```

This will give us a visualization that looks something like this:

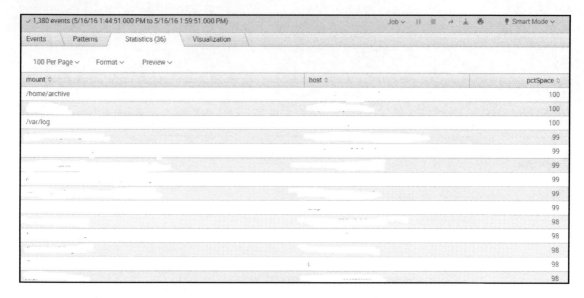

Be aware of what you set your time range to, as the report is quite dependent on this. If you want this to run once a day, then set the time range picker to 24 hours.

Once we have that search, we simply click on the **Save As** feature:

Click **Report**, and pick a name for this report:

To view this report, simply go to the **Reports** menu:

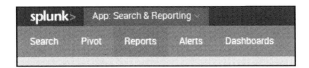

And select your newly saved report to have it populate for you through your time range:

From here, you have the option to export, print, or embed these reports, or even send them manually to a person or group of people.

A report is not meant to be triggered in an automated fashion, as this is part of the alert functionality in Splunk.

 Make sure you have your permissions for this report set properly, or the users you send this report to will not be able to view it!

From here, we can accelerate these reports. Report acceleration is helpful when attempting to get large sets of results to return faster, as it summarizes the data and stores it in virtual memory. We do this by clicking on the **Edit** function, and clicking **Edit Acceleration**:

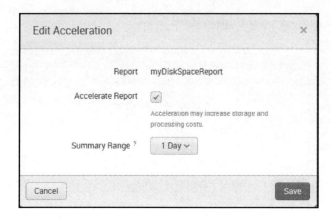

We will then need to choose how long we want the historical data to show, which in this case is a **1 Day** period, and click **Save**.

If we choose, we can then stick these reports in a dashboard, and start off with a good, fast-loading panel.

Dashboards

Dashboards are the culmination of all of the previous things we've discussed concerning knowledge objects, search queries, and reports. These are the things that everybody loves, and truly provide the most value to your user base when made correctly. In short, a dashboard is a collection of searches and/or reports framed inside HTML in different panels.

Dashboarding can be an art form in itself; however, I'm going to suggest that we stick to the basics until people start seeing the value in the Splunk product. Most of what you will need can be downloaded and pulled from the **Dashboard Examples** app; these are some of the techniques that we will be talking about here in this chapter.

The link to this app is here: `https://splunkbase.splunk.com/app/163/`.

There are a few different types of dashboard to be aware of.

Form-based

These types of dashboard allow input from a user in order to filter the downstream panels for relevant information. In short, if you want to see a single machine you can type in the name, and only that machine's data populates.

Drilldown

Drilldown dashboards add another layer of complexity, but provide a lot of value by easing the navigation of data. These are the dashboards that are clickable, and each link you click takes you to a view that is more granular than the previous one, effectively drilling into your data for root cause analysis.

Report/data model-based

Report/data model-based dashboards leverage summary-level information in order to enhance performance while still giving high-level information. These are usually the most complex type of dashboard, but in some cases their results can be automated to send a whole dashboard to an email distribution list in PDF format, which eases weekly reporting. These are also the fastest populating type of dashboards.

Search-based

While this is the slowest out of the bunch, this is also probably the most common of all of dashboard types. This dashboard has multiple panels, with a unique search set in all of them. Let's say we have a dashboard with 12 panels set up this way. Each of those searches has to run and complete before that panel populates, and none of those searches are accessing summary-level data. They are each searching the raw data before results can be displayed, so this is the equivalent of running 12 searches at the same time, every time this dashboard loads, slowing down the display of these results until each search finishes.

In order to not go down the rabbit hole that is Splunk development, we are going to stick to simplified XML, form-based dashboards.

Modules

Splunk's **Simplified XML** is basically XML with JavaScript at the backend. Splunk lovingly refers to these JavaScripts as **extensions** when one is needed for a specific function. In simplified XML, they have some basic modules that someone can access in order to create a dashboard with ease by pointing and clicking, instead of having to know all the advanced XML to render a page.

Each module has a series of tokens that can pass data values down to an underlying search, or even be put in a link to a URL. These become very important in Splunk development in order to display the appropriate information and filter on the click of a button.

There are a few different module types.

Data input

Data input modules are things that add or filter data within a Splunk dashboard. The most common is the time range picker module, which adds the length of time a dashboard will search. There are others such as text input, radio button, check box, drop down, and multi-select to name a few. These are the basis for form-based dashboards.

Chart

This module is the base of any **chart**, **timechart**, or anything similar, and renders a chart in any form in Splunk.

Table

The table module is the module that renders data in the form of a table. Often this is the result set of a | `stats` command, or a | `table` command, but it can render results in other functions such as **xyseries**, as we've discussed in previous chapters.

Single value

This is a module commonly used to show counts of things, or averages of things within a single value. This module can also show labels, or descriptions, and it shows this in a large font on your dashboard.

Map module

This module is the one that displays the world map, or the map of the US, or EMEA with little pie graphs in different locations. This module is very powerful for looking at a data set that contains locational information, and rendering it specific to anywhere on the globe.

Tokens

Tokens are at the heart of searching and passing data from one module to another, or one page to another. These are the objects within Splunk that allow you to pass values of a field or result set to another module. These are often represented by the symbol `$foo$` in the documentation. Something to keep in mind is that for each module the tokens are often different. This is also where we reach into the development world to understand how these work.

For now, I am going to focus on the tokens of the contextual and dynamic drill-down, in order to give context to what we will be learning in this chapter.

There are far too many tokens within Splunk to list, however they are all necessary. This is basically how they work. A token is set as part of an input, which is then passed to a search in order to filter data to the visualization as represented through the following screenshot:

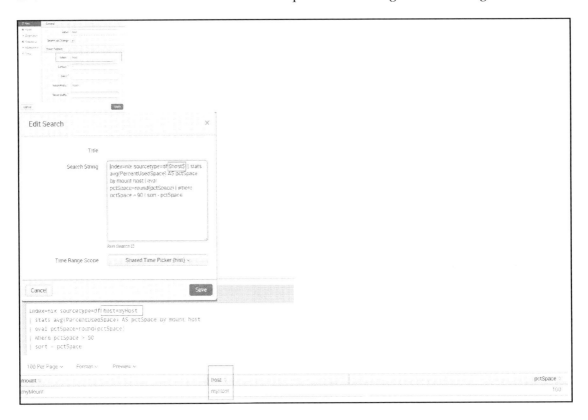

Once set, this token can be used by other searches downstream with the use of the `$<token>$` characters.

Alternatively, some tokens are hard-coded into modules, in order to pass data to other dashboards. Here is a list of tokens that are available for passing data to another view:

Token	Description
`$click.name$`	Name of the leftmost field that appears in a table.
`$click.value$`	Value of the leftmost column in the row.
`$click.name2$`	Name of the column.
`$click.value2$`	Value of the column.
`$row.<fieldname>$`	All field values for the table row.
`$earliest$/$latest$`	Time range of the search.

The tokens we will focus on in this section are the ones that are set within the UI portion of Splunk, which allow for contextual drilldowns. These very basic tokens are easily visible and defined by whatever value you select.

They are also important, because it is how we can start to filter data within a basic dashboard in order to refine what our users are seeing within their dashboard. This is basically giving them a bit of control, while removing the confusing search syntax.

Building a form-based dashboard

The first part of a form-based dashboard is deciding which inputs our users will care about, and usually this starts with the time range picker module.

Let's create a dashboard out of the report we made earlier from Linux `df` data. When we open up our report, we notice that there is a useful option in the top right-hand section **Add to Dashboard**:

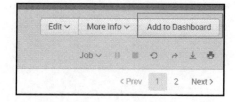

When we click on that button we get this popup, and we have to choose a name for it:

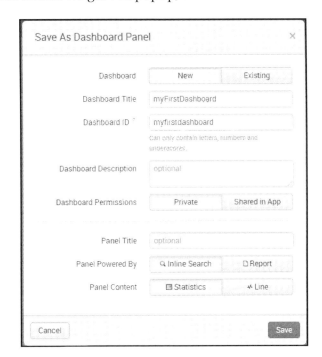

In this case, I choose myFirstDashboard, and click **Save**.

On the next popup, just click **View Dashboard** and Splunk will take you right to it.

Now we understand that our report gives us data for a single day on all machines, and some of our users would like to be able to see data for last week as well, as only a single host is experiencing errors.

The easiest way to do this is by adding the time range picker, and a **Text** module, then set their tokens to be passed down to the original search. This will allow the user to select the time, and the machine they would like to see data for within their dashboard.

To do this, click on the **Edit** button in the top right-hand section of your dashboard; then click the **+ Add Input** button; and select **Time**:

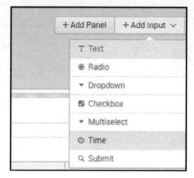

Doing so will give you the time range picker module in the top left. Click on the little pencil icon, and you will then see some options to set:

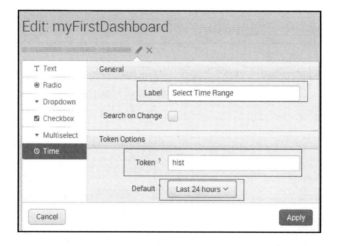

The label is what the user will see in the field while the **Token** is the name of the token that will be passed to underlying searches. Both of these fields are arbitrary and can be set to whatever you like.

The **Default** section is the default time range to be selected and searched. Splunk defaults to all time, which in this case is far too dense a search, so best practice is to always limit your data set to a single day, or 24 hours, and let the user decide what they want to see by changing the time range if need be.

Once you have changed these options, go to your search panel, click the magnifying glass icon, and select **Edit Search String**:

From here, you will see the option to adjust the search time range in the **Time Range Scope** portion of the popup. Make sure to select the token from your time range picker from here:

One that is set up, we just need to set up the text input field. We do this by going to the **+ Add Input** menu again, and selecting **Text**:

We then go to the pencil icon on that module and begin editing the options there as well:

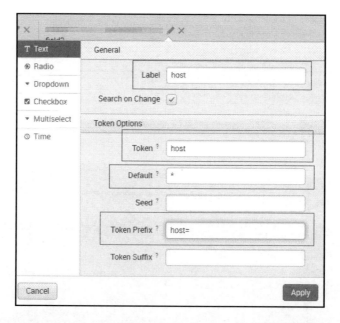

As you can see, some similar items need to be set within this module.

The **Label** is the text above the box itself, the token is arbitrary, the **Default** is best set to * to include all results, and then the token prefix is any characters you would like to precede the value being passed to the underlying searches. In this case, we are passing the characters for host=.

When we click **Apply**, we notice that our description has changed, but in order for it to take effect we also need to adjust our search to accommodate this token.

So when we go back into the **Edit Search** string of our panel, we use the token name surrounded by dollar signs to tell Splunk to expect a value from an upstream module.

Since we are using the field host, it's best to insert that into the root part of the search, so that's what we can do here:

Because we added the prefix characters, Splunk will add the `host=<value>` to the search, and our search results will be filtered by whichever host our users wanted to see.

To take this a step further, let's say that now our users also want to see CPU and MEM metrics from their host as well.

We already have the searches from our previous examples for these metrics, so all we need to do is add some panels and adjust them to receive the right tokens. Click on **Edit** at the top right and then **Add Panel**. Select **New** | **Line** for each of these and make the same adjustment as we did before.

Here is the CPU search:

```
index=os sourcetype=cpu cpu=all | eval cpu=(100 - pctIdle) | timechart
avg(cpu) by host
```

And this is the MEM search:

```
index=nix sourcetype=freeMem | eval mem=(realfreeMem / totMemory) * 100 |
timechart avg(mem) by host
```

All we have to do is change the root search for the CPU panel to accept the tokens:

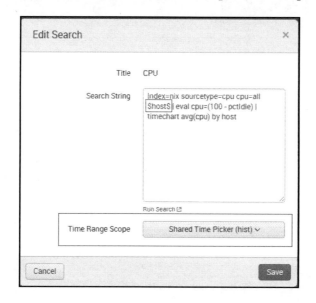

And then for the memory panel, to do the same:

Then label each panel appropriately, and we have a basic host level dashboard for OS-level metrics:

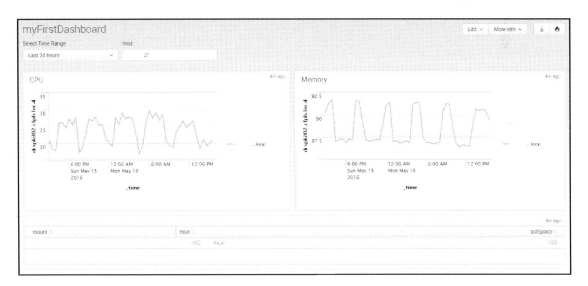

Summary

In this chapter, we have discussed how to create form-based dashboards leveraging foo variables as selectors to appropriately pass information to another search, or another dashboard; also, we have seen how to create an effective drilldown effect. In the next chapter, we will see how to optimize dashboards to increase performance. This ultimately affects how quickly dashboards load results. To do this, we can adjust search queries, leverage summary indexes, the KV store, accelerated searches, and data models to name a few.

8
Search Optimization

When we create dashboards quickly, we often create dashboards with existing searches with a different field or displaying a different set of stats results. In this chapter, we will discuss how to optimize these searches for performance in a dashboard as well as how to leverage things such as reports or data models in order to speed up your load times.

In this chapter, we will discuss the following topics:

- Form dashboard optimizations
  - Root search variables
  - Evaluation variables
  - Filter variables
- Using base searches
  - Post-process functions
- Using reports to speed up dashboards
  - Referencing summary results from a report
- Creating a data model
  - Referencing a data model in your search

Types of dashboard search panel

In Splunk, each panel within a dashboard can be one of a series of types. Designing your dashboard virtually before you implement it, leveraging some of these panels, is very helpful in creating optimized performance. The architecture of your dashboard and which search queries you decide to use directly relate to the performance of your dashboard.

Raw data search panel

This is a search panel with a single query in it that searches raw data each time the dashboard loads. This is usually the fastest way of creating dashboards; however, the more of these panels you add to your dashboard, the slower the performance.

Shared search panel (base search)

These are also sometimes referred to as **post-process** panels. These panels reference a single root search hidden within the XML source code of the page and then perform a function such as **stats** or **timechart**on the results. This assists performance by allowing the dashboard to load by running only a single search to populate all the panels on the page. The catch is that with this kind of search, you are limited to ten thousand results, as a post-process can't accept more than that.

Report reference panel

These panels reference a saved and scheduled search, accessing less raw data. A popular way to leverage this is to have the base search in a dashboard (as mentioned previously) reference a schedule search and then use post processes to manipulate the data. This increases performance twofold, by referencing only the scheduled search results and using those results to power all the panels in your dashboard only once.

Data model/pivot reference panels

These will be panels that reference a data model, which has been built previously, or a pivot. In much the same way as the report reference, you can refer to a created data model, except here you can pull out specific results from the data model. This is the most performance efficient way to show dashboards; however, it is not always needed or sometimes not applicable.

Raw data search

The first thing to note about form dashboard optimizations is that the closer to the root search you can place tokens, the faster your searches will go, meaning that if we use our dashboard inputs to place tokens such as **host source, source type, eventtype,** or **tag** within the root search, then we will increase the performance of our searches.

For instance, let's take some dashboards from an app and break them down. I am going to choose the **Citrix netscaler** app because it's simplistic enough in nature. I'm going to use the **Load Balancing Dashboard** as the single page of focus within this app.

```
https://splunkbase.splunk.com/app/370/
```

The dashboard looks like the following screenshot:

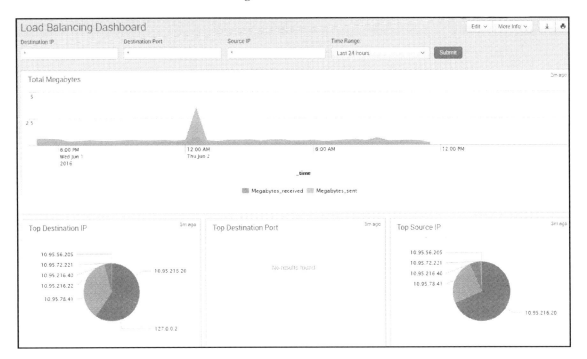

Notice that, when we start delving into each of the modules, there are three text inputs, one time input, and a single **Submit** button at the top of the page. I will focus on the text inputs and the tokens they are passing for now.

Looking closer at each input, you will notice that each token has the option of a prefix, and a suffix, as shown in the following screenshot:

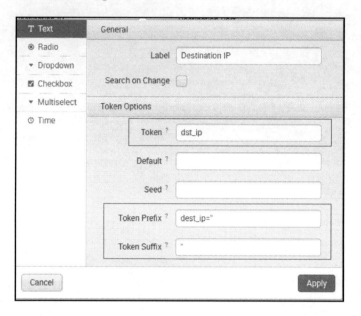

The prefix/suffix simply ease the development of dashboards, shortening what one needs to apply to each dashboard panel search query.

In the **Total Megabytes** panel, we can see that we are using an **eventtype**, then a string, and then our tokens in order to formulate this search panel, as shown in the following screenshot:

In the preceding instance, the tokens are placed in the root search, optimizing the search times for individual panels that search raw data as much as possible. You will also notice that the only thing we need to add is the token itself instead of **src_ip=src_ip**. This is because of the prefix and suffix that have been set within the inputs. If you do not populate the prefix/suffix options in your data input section, then please use the full **src_ip=src_ip** option in your query syntax in your dashboards.

This effectively changes the dashboard to something into which someone can simply plug an IP or port, click **Submit**, and have the data they are looking for:

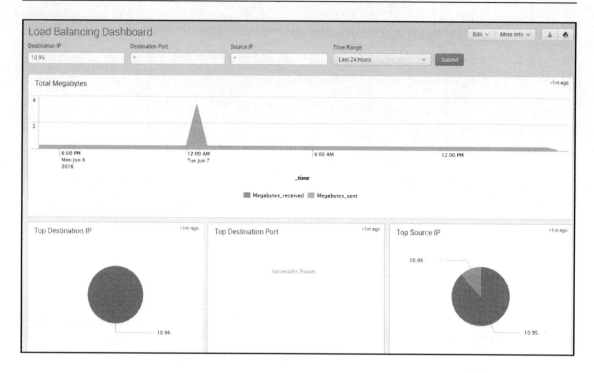

You will notice that each of the other panels has a similar setup, where the tokens are part of the root search and the panel itself is set to a global time range picker.

There is something to note about this dashboard though. All of these searches are independent of each other, so every time this dashboard loads it will be running four concurrent searches. This can become problematic when you have 20 users trying to open a dashboard like this at the same time. This is why Splunk has made alternate ways of making these searches happen.

Shared searching using a base search

To affect how many searches we kick off at one time, we can ask our panels in Splunk to refer to a base search that starts when the dashboard loads. The base search is hidden; however, the results will be displayed on the panels within the dashboard and we can still use our tokens within the search as well. You will have to go into the XML to do this, but it's often worth the performance increase.

I recommend downloading an app called **Splunk 6.x Dashboard Examples**. This will give you a great start; you will find some great tools to help you create some basic and even more advanced dashboards.

I will be using the preceding example app and referencing the techniques in the **Recursive Search Post-process** section of the Splunk 6.x Dashboard Examples.

 Post-process searches are limited to 10,000 results. Anything with a timechart will almost always have more results than that.

In our previous example, all of the panels use the same data to populate their charts; however, the only panel that is not compatible with this technique is the **Total Megabytes** panel. Why, you ask? Because if someone sets the time range to something with more than 10,000 data points, they will come to you (the Splunk admin) and say it is broken because nothing is populating. See the preceding note.

For this example, we will focus on the bottom three panels, as they are compatible with this technique, as all three panels show only the top 10 in each:

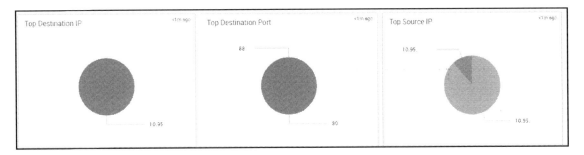

If you open the **Edit | show source** menu, you will see the underlying XML, which will have all of the searches and tokens that you will need for this example:

```
    <chart>
        <title>Top Destination IP</title>
        <search>
          <query>eventtype=netscaler TCP $dst_ip$  $src_ip$ | top
dest_ip</query>
        </search>
        <option name="charting.chart">pie</option>
    </chart>
  <chart>
        <title>Top Destination Port</title>
        <search>
          <query>eventtype=netscaler TCP $dst_ip$ $dst_port$ $src_ip$ | top
dest_port</query>
```

```
        </search>
        <option name="charting.chart">pie</option>
        <option name="charting.legend.placement">bottom</option>
    </chart>
     <chart>
        <title>Top Source IP</title>
        <search>
          <query>eventtype=netscaler TCP $dst_ip$  $src_ip$ | top
src_ip</query>
        </search>
        <option name="charting.chart">pie</option>
        <option name="charting.legend.placement">bottom</option>
</chart>
```

I have removed quite a bit of extra code due to space restrictions.

You will see that each chart begins with a `<query>` statement, which will be the part we need to focus on in order to adjust our searches after we create our base search.

Creating a base search

At the very top of the XML of any dashboard panel, we have the option to create a base search to reference in later panels of the dashboard.

In our case, we will create `netscaler` events on those references.

Following is the XML as well as the root search query we would use in order to get all of the `netscaler` events with a single search and to pass those results to our child panels:

```
<form>
    <!-- Global search to populate everything in the panel -->
    <search id="baseSearch">
        <query>eventtype=netscaler TCP | fields _time src_ip dest_ip
src_port dest_port</query>
        <earliest>-1h@h</earliest>
        <latest>@h</latest>
    </search>
```

You will notice that when we call the search module, we are also giving it an id called `baseSearch`.

We have structured the search in such a way that we will only see the data in the fields that we have referenced. If we were to remove the `|fields _time src_ip` portion of this search, then all of the fields would be present; however, the search would take slightly longer to complete. More data is equal to more time till completion.

Referencing a base search

We reference our base search in each child panel that needs to display counts or averages of any of the fields we populated in our base search.

Following is the XML that we will use to reference our base search in all of our child panels that will use this data:

```
<chart>
    <title>Top Destination IP</title>
    <search base="baseSearch">
      <query>search $dst_ip$  $src_ip$ | top dest_ip</query>
    </search>
    <option name="charting.chart">pie</option>
</chart>
<chart>
    <title>Top Destination Port</title>
    <search base="baseSearch">
      <query>search $dst_ip$ $dst_port$ $src_ip$ | top dest_port</query>
    </search>
    <option name="charting.chart">pie</option>
    <option name="charting.legend.placement">bottom</option>
</chart>
 <chart>
    <title>Top Source IP</title>
    <search base="baseSearch">
      <query>search $dst_ip$  $src_ip$ | top src_ip</query>
    </search>
    <option name="charting.chart">pie</option>
    <option name="charting.legend.placement">bottom</option>
</chart>
```

Now notice that, when we call each chart module, there is a new option called `base="baseSearch"`. This option references the results of the search with `id="baseSearch"` within the dashboard.

After we have successfully referenced the results of our base search, we will then need to perform another quick search for each of our tokens so that we can filter the base result set even more when a user adds the right input.

This will effectively make the three panels in the preceding dashboard populate at the same time, as they are referencing the same data, and using this technique we have also reduced the number of concurrent searches on that single dashboard to two instead of four. This increases the amount of users that can access this dashboard at one time, while also increasing the dashboard population performance.

Report referenced panels

The panels start to increase the efficiency of Splunk's visualizations considerably, and the reason is quite simple. A scheduled report is held in cache memory, and that data can then be referenced by search panels in order to streamline your user experience. A report is little more than a saved search that is scheduled to run at specific intervals; because that report continues to refresh its result set, the panels that reference that data can display those results that much faster.

I will be referencing the examples used in the Splunk 6.x Dashboard Examples, so for future referencing please feel free to check out that app.

Let's use our same dashboard example to explore how this will work. I am going to ask you to use your imagination a bit for this one in order to understand the technique.

Let's say for a moment that, in our Splunk instance, our Netscaler is doing Gbps worth of throughput and it is taking a very long time to generate the chart from the first panel, which our security engineers have complained about. They have simple stated that Splunk is slow and needs to be fixed while referencing this chart.

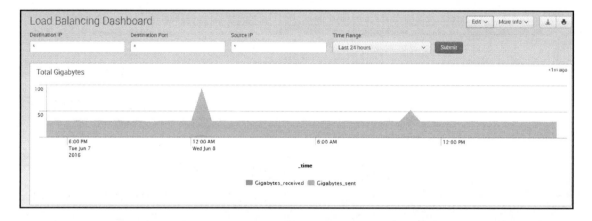

There are a series of things a Splunk admin can say in order to help them understand why this dashboard is slow; however, foregoing those, we will simply leverage the report referenced dashboard panel in order to resolve this issue for our security team.

The first thing to do is to open up the dashboard panel's search query and save it as a report. To do so, click on the magnifying glass on the bottom left (mouse over it, as it is hidden), as shown in the following screenshot:

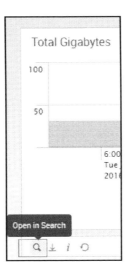

This will explode the full query into a search bar that so you can see what you are dealing with.

Since this is the only panel we will be applying this report to, we will adjust the query to remove the presentation aspect first and then simply click on the **Save As** menu and then **Report**. The reason for this is that, because we will need to filter this search by src/dest IP's, we want the raw data. The timechart portion of this search removes the src_ip and dest_ip fields, so we lose the ability to filter on them if applied.

In short, this following is the search you will see for your report:

```
eventtype=netscaler TCP dest_ip="*"  src_ip="*" | bin _time span=5m | eval
tbrmb=Total_bytes_recv/(1024*1024*1024)| eval
tbsmb=Total_bytes_send/(1024*1024*1024)
```

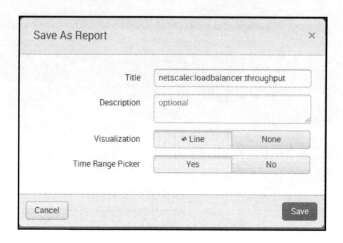

In the preceding menu, you will see that there is no option to choose your time range. This means that whatever time range you have selected will be saved to the report, unless you add the **time range picker** module to your report.

Whatever time range you have in your query will be what is presented on your dashboard. You will not be able to adjust the time range of your report from your dashboard time range picker module.

Once we've saved the report, click on the **View** button in order to view it. Once there, click on the **Edit** menu, select **Acceleration**, and then select the historical summary of the chart, as shown in the following screenshot. Most people don't need to go back more than 30 days, so it's a safe starting point.

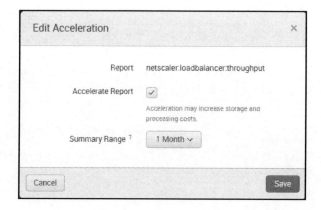

Now that we have our report saved, as well as accelerated, we can go back to the dashboard where we want to place it, and reference it in order to speed up the search.

Navigate back to your dashboard (in this case the Netscaler load balancing dashboard), and go to the source XML by clicking on **Edit** and then on **Edit Source**.

Like referencing a base search, we are going to reference the report in a hidden search as well. The following is our XML:

```
<search id="throughput" ref="netscaler:loadbalancer:throughput" />
  <row>
    <chart>
      <title>Total Gigabytes</title>
      <search base="throughput">
      </search>
      <option name="charting.chart">area</option>
      <option name="charting.legend.placement">bottom</option>
      <option name="charting.primaryAxisTitle.text">Time</option>
      <option name="charting.secondaryAxisTitle.text">MegaBytes</option>
      <option
name="charting.axisLabelsX.majorLabelStyle.overflowMode">ellipsisNone</opti
on>
      <option
name="charting.axisLabelsX.majorLabelStyle.rotation">0</option>
      <option name="charting.axisTitleX.visibility">visible</option>
      <option name="charting.axisTitleY.visibility">visible</option>
      <option name="charting.axisTitleY2.visibility">visible</option>
      <option name="charting.axisX.scale">linear</option>
      <option name="charting.axisY.scale">linear</option>
      <option name="charting.axisY2.enabled">false</option>
      <option name="charting.axisY2.scale">inherit</option>
      <option name="charting.chart.bubbleMaximumSize">50</option>
      <option name="charting.chart.bubbleMinimumSize">10</option>
      <option name="charting.chart.bubbleSizeBy">area</option>
      <option name="charting.chart.nullValueMode">gaps</option>
      <option name="charting.chart.sliceCollapsingThreshold">0.01</option>
      <option name="charting.chart.stackMode">default</option>
      <option name="charting.chart.style">shiny</option>
      <option name="charting.drilldown">all</option>
      <option name="charting.layout.splitSeries">0</option>
      <option
name="charting.legend.labelStyle.overflowMode">ellipsisMiddle</option>
    </chart>
  </row>
```

At the top of the preceding code, you will notice the reference to a hidden search with an ID of `throughput`, which is then referenced by the underlying chart module in order to display the results.

After that is completed, add the filtering tokens for src / dst _ip and the presentation portion back into your dashboard panel, as shown in the following screenshot:

The time range won't matter, as it is set by the report you saved and are referencing in the XML.

At the end of it all, the XML will look something like the following:

```
<search id="throughput" ref="netscaler:loadbalancer:throughput"></search>
  <row>
    <chart>
      <title>Total Gigabytes</title>
      <search base="throughput">
        <query>| search $src_ip$ $dst_ip$  | timechart sum(tbrmb) as
Gigabytes_received sum(tbsmb) as Gigabytes_sent</query>
      </search>
```

Now add whatever other options you would like to see.

The final result is a dashboard panel(s) that populates very quickly due to being accelerated/scheduled as a report.

Data model/pivot referenced panels

A data model is a fantastic way to speed up dashboards, and it can handle some very complex data and make it understandable. The Pivot function relies on a data model in order to generate the visualization. If at all possible, these are the ways to build dashboards in order to pull lots of data to the surface of Splunk efficiently.

I will skip the best practices of data model creation; you should refer to the following link if you want to know how to create a data model: http://docs.splunk.com/Documentation/Splunk/latest/PivotTutorial/WelcometothePivotTutorial.

Once our data model is created, we can very easily reference it within our dashboards through pivots and save those pivot charts as panels.

To do so, go the data model itself and click on the **tcp** constraint for your data model, as shown in the following screenshot:

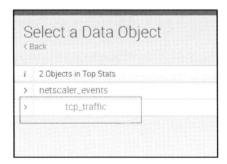

When you select this object, make sure you click the pie icon on the bottom left, as shown in the next screenshot:

And select the time range (24 hours) and the color filter of your choice. In this case, I will be using the field `dest_ip`. That will give us a pie chart that looks exactly like the one in the dashboard, as shown in the next screenshot:

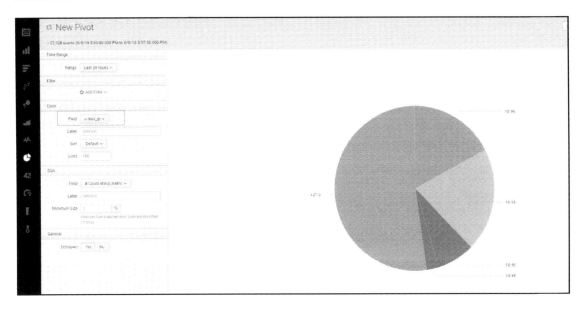

When you have this, simply click on **Save As** and **Dashboard Panel** at the top right-hand side of the page:

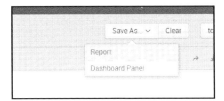

Since in this example we are simply replacing the current panels with data model-driven panels, we can select the existing dashboard called **Load Balancing Dashboard**, name our panel **Top Dest IP's**, and then click on **Save**, as shown in the next screenshot:

That will add this data model-driven panel to our dashboard at the bottom of the page. Do this for the rest of the panels as well, and in the end you should have something that looks like the following screenshot:

Go through and change the new data model-driven panels so they use the time range picker on our dashboard:

And then delete the old panels. Now you have data model driven panels in the netscaler apps dashboard.

Special notes

Keep in mind that, with both the report-driven dashboard panels and the data model/pivot-driven dashboard panels, making them use tokens is possible; however, it takes some massaging of the syntax.

The techniques in this chapter can be applied to any dashboard that is leveraging simplified XML, which most dashboards on Splunkbase use. If you already have an app installed that is experiencing some performance issues, try one of these techniques to see if you can improve the performance for your users.

Summary

In this chapter, you learnt how to optimize dashboards to increase performance. This ultimately affects how quickly dashboards load results. We did this by adjusting search queries, leveraging summary indexes, and using the KV Store, accelerated searches, and data models to name a few. In the next chapter, we will discuss how to take a series of apps from Splunkbase, as well as any user-created dashboard, and put them into a Splunk app for ease of use. You will also learn how to adjust navigation XML to ease user navigation of such an app.

9
App Creation and Consolidation

In this chapter, we will focus on how to not only create an app, but also to add functionality to it by consolidating functions from other apps on Splunk base. The advantage to this is that it enables users to leverage operations such as a **Lightweight Directory Access Protocol (LDAP)** search, or a different event type in a custom app that is being created for a proprietary purpose. You can also create apps in context with the data that is being viewed, and all knowledge objects can be permissioned appropriately. Maybe you want to create an app for your engineering staff for Windows and Linux, and you don't want to clutter your *launcher* page with any more apps because you've installed a plethora of them already. I'm going to show you some techniques for how to do this at the indexing and search head levels, so that you can keep your administrative overhead as low as possible. We will learn about:

- Types of app:
    - Search app
    - Deployment app
    - Indexer/cluster app
    - Technical add-on (TA)
    - Supporting add-on (SA)
    - Premium apps

- Consolidating search apps:
    - Creating a custom app
    - App migrations
    - Knowledge object consolidation
    - Search app navigation

- Consolidating indexing/forwarding apps:
    - Forwarding apps
    - Indexer/cluster apps

Types of apps

An app will be called something different depending on which tier it is placed on. Splunk would have you believe that there are only two types of apps: apps and add-ons. However those of you that have used Splunk for a while know that this is simply not true. Using general terminology, an app is something that goes on a search head, whereas an add-on is something that could go on almost any component of Splunk depending on its purpose. It can be quite confusing if you're just stepping into the Splunk world and someone says *Let's install <insert app name here> app*, and god forbid if someone says *Let's install the enterprise security app*, and they task you (a new(ish) admin) with its installation.

Search apps

This type of apps are deployed on the search head only, and primarily comprises knowledge objects. These are event types, lookup files, field extractions, and the like, as well as all the .xml files that make up the actual dashboards. This is the visualization component of the data, and will not work if the data is nonexistent or parsed incorrectly. The collected dashboards are usually what people see in pictures (all populated of course), and they are important to releasing the value of Splunk.

Deployment apps

These apps go on the forwarding tier of your Splunk deployment, and usually comprise data inputs. Most of these will have a series of data inputs, and some specialized props.conf and transforms.conf settings to adjust the data pre-index time.

Indexer/cluster apps

These apps are made up of all of the knowledge objects that will parse the data pre-index time, and add any relevant indexes to your indexer/index clustering tier. These apps pave the road for the deployment apps to send data, and get it into the right format on disk for Splunk.

Technical add-ons

These apps are usually used in addition to a search app in order to set up data inputs and add any indexes/knowledge objects to each tier. In some instances, they can be deployed to all the tiers in a Splunk instance (**Forwarding/Indexing/Searching**); however to know which tiers to deploy these apps to, read the documentation.

Supporting add-ons

These usually support a larger search app in some context. The one that comes to my mind is the LDAP search SA for the Windows infrastructure app. The LDAP search SA is a custom script, written by Splunk, to query your domain server for a series of data. It is used as a custom command, and it is only necessary for the Windows infrastructure app to populate a handful of dashboards. The supporting add on apps usually add additional functionality such as a custom command, or an API call that is required to populate a dashboard within a search app. There can be other reasons, so read the documentation before installation.

Premium apps

These apps are extraordinarily difficult to set up, and get configured. They are called premium because Splunk will recommend that you have a professional services consultant come on site in order to set this app up. As an example, the **Enterprise Security App (ESA)** is a premium app. These apps *can* be installed by a knowledgeable Splunk admin; however, if you don't have some years of experience in this, get Professional Services to come and install it. These are not easy apps to configure, and it requires a lot of tweaking to get them to work right. It may be expensive, but you will save yourself a monster headache. These kinds of app often have a series of other apps that they depend on, so usually you don't install just the ESA (for instance); there are three other apps (at least) that need to be installed to even begin configuring this app to work.

Consolidating search apps

Consolidating search apps starts to come in handy when we want to begin to develop the ever-elusive **single pane of glass**. There is usually a very large amount of data gathered in Splunk, though many people create disparate apps for a unique purpose. Take for instance a *Network* app that has all router/firewall/switch logs, and then an Active Directory app that has all Microsoft Active Directory data, as well as a Juniper SRX app in order to pay attention to the Quality Assurance environment. While these provide value to a user, the visualization often gets cumbersome on login as you have logs of different apps and titles to sift through to find the data you want to see. App consolidation is a great way to make everything available with a single click, and then a user just navigates to the appropriate set of dashboards.

Creating a custom app

To begin the consolidation process, it's best to start by creating a custom app. The process is quite easy, and there are a couple of ways to go about this. Truthfully, knowing the best method in which to create it will depend on the type of app you are creating. In short, an app is a directory with a specific file structure, containing specific files that Splunk is looking for in order to process, and that's all. Apply all relevant knowledge objects there, permission them within the app, and you have a single spot to view your data.

To create a custom search app, log in to your search head and go to **Manage Apps** as shown in the following screenshot:

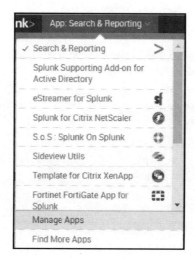

Then click on the **Create app** button, as shown in the following screenshot:

Name your app, and then click **Save**, and you will have yourself a new app. You can choose to apply a template if you like; however, using the **barebones** template will give you a solid baseline.

When you look in the folder, you will see the folder that you created, which represents the app:

In this folder you can add all necessary configs and knowledge objects to formalize your data. You can also consolidate functions such as time wrap or an LDAP search in these folders as well.

It's that easy to make an app. The hard part comes in configuring all of the knowledge objects and consolidating them all to make them work.

App migrations

So, now that we have our app (my_app), we can begin to consolidate dashboards and knowledge objects by migrating them into this app. This technique will apply to many of the apps on Splunkbase. This does NOT apply to premium apps (ESA, ITSI, and others).

Let's say (for instance) that you want a single place to view both Windows and Linux operational data (CPU, MEM, disk, and others), but you like some of the dashboards that either app has out-of-the-box. The first step is to consolidate all of the knowledge objects into your app on the search head. Doing this can be as easy as performing a copy/paste and then restarting the search head. It can also get much more complicated, so I will show you a few simple techniques that will work with the majority of apps out there.

Knowledge objects

In the `Splunk_TA_win` (`https://splunkbase.splunk.com/app/742/`) you will note that it has a familiar file structure. Navigate to the `Splunk_TA_windows/default` directory. Here you will need a few files, and this will hold true for any app that you want to migrate:

File Name	Contents
`Props.conf`	Contains all field-extractions and transform calls, auto-lookups, and calculated fields for the app.
`Transforms.conf`	This has all necessary transformations of the data, or field reports for the app.
`Eventtypes.conf`	This contains all event summaries for searches within the app.
`Macros.conf`	This contains all unique search definitions or filters that are referenced by the app.
Lookups (all files)	This folder (`<app_name>/lookups`) will contain all necessary lookup files relevant to the app.
`Savedsearches.conf`	This will contain all saved searches for any dashboard within the app, as well as any lookup generating searches and alerts.

For this example, we will keep our scope limited to just these files for now. App consolidation can require a lot more than just these four files, though these are very important to get data out of your searches.

When you're copying the contents of each of these files, it's usually best to mark it with a delimiter in the file. I've used ASCII art in the past, as shown in the following screenshot, but a simple comment line will do, announcing what the contents of that section are. Nice!

```
##################################################################################
###      _   _     ___   _   _    ___     _____     __   _   _ _____  _____   ###
###     / \ \ \   / / | | \ | |  | _ \   / _ \ \   / /  \ \ / /|  ___|/  ___|   ###
###    | |  \ \ / /| | |  \| |  | | | | | | | \ \_/ /    \ V / | |__  \ `--.    ###
###    | |   \ V / | | | . ` |  | | | | | | | |\   /      \ /  |  __|  `--. \   ###
###    | |    | |  | | | |\  |  | |_| | | |_| | | |        | |  | |___ /\__/ /   ###
###     \_/\  \_/  |_| |_| \_|   \___/   \___/  |_|        \_/  \____/ \____/    ###
###        \/              \/           \/          \/         \/               ###
### Windows OS                                                                  ###
##################################################################################

#########################
### WEB / IIS Logs ###
#########################

[iis]
EXTRACT-iis_host = W3SVC(2|3)\s(?<iis_host>\w+)\s
EXTRACT-website = \d+\.\d+\.\d+\.\d+\s\w+\s\/(?<website>\w+)
FIELDALIAS-useragent = cs_User_Agent as http_user_agent
#LOOKUP-uri = uri_lookup.csv uri_root AS uri_root
```

This is an example of a section header within the `props.conf` file for all Windows settings. The same will be true of our Linux section header, and this will be in each file in our preceding list.

Dashboard consolidation

When consolidating dashboards, there are a few ways to do this:

- Copy all `.xml` files from the source app to your app (folder to folder in the shell)
- Copy the XML directly using the UI
- Copy the searches within the dashboard, modify them to your data, and implement them in your app

For this example I will use the third option, as the Windows app has a series of custom modules and HTML that doesn't allow us to copy directly from one folder to another without a long process of discovery. We are going for simple and effective here.

Let's use the Splunk app for the Windows infrastructure's dashboard called **Performance Monitoring,** shown in the following screenshot:

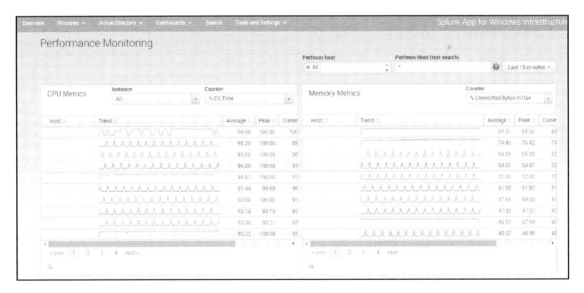

This dashboard has been created with a series of custom modules that have been written by Splunk, which we can't easily copy/paste. It's mostly formatting at the end of the day; however in this case let's say we don't care about that, and we want to apply this to our app using simplified XML. So let's break this dashboard down into its fundamentals, as shown in the following screenshot:

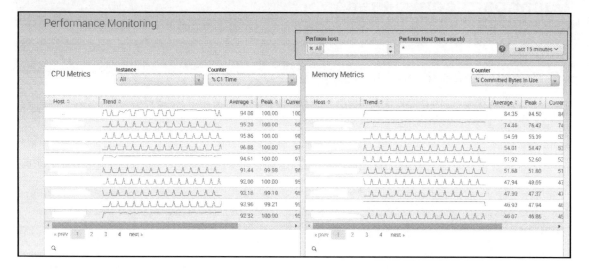

In the preceding screenshot we can see there are three global data inputs, and then two data inputs in the **CPU Metrics** panel, and another one in the **Memory Metrics** panel.

Let's start by creating a new dashboard in our app with the three global inputs. When we create our dashboard, we go to **Add Input** and add the following three modules:

- Multi-select
- Text box
- Time range picker

And we label them the same as our Windows app, as shown in the following screenshot:

Because the multi-select auto-populates, we will need to set a search in order to make that a reality. Common sense tells us that we want to search perfmon data for the host names within the last 15 minutes or so, so that's the search we will set.

That search looks like this:

```
Index=perfmon | stats count by host | sort + host
```

We place that in the multi select:

We will get all of the host names within that index for the last 15 minutes, sorted alphabetically.

Now we need to create the panels and the other inputs for CPU.

To get the search, just navigate to the Windows app performance monitoring dashboard and click the little magnifying glass in the bottom left corner, shown in the following screenshot:

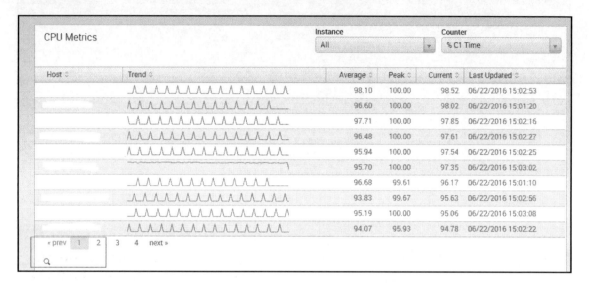

That will launch the following search:

```
eventtype="perfmon_windows" (Host="*") Host="*" object="Processor"
counter="% C1 Time" instance="*"
| stats sparkline(avg(Value)) as Trend avg(Value) as Average, max(Value) as
Peak, latest(Value) as Current, latest(_time) as "Last Updated" by Host
| convert ctime("Last Updated")
| sort - Current
| eval Average=round(Average, 2)
| eval Peak=round(Peak, 2)
| eval Current=round(Current, 2)
```

Just create a new statistics panel and, if you have all of your knowledge objects copied correctly, you should see the panel populate. Now we only need to add the instance/counter data inputs for this panel. If you don't see the panel populate, just make adjustments to the root search as needed. (`index=perfmon` instead of `eventtype="perfmon windows"`).

First we will add two drop-down data inputs, and pull them into our panel as shown in the following screenshot:

These two inputs are also auto-populated, and if we apply a bit of common sense we can also figure that out. We are just looking for a list of instances and counters over the last 15 minutes, and we need them in a drop-down menu.

We also need to make sure we start to number our tokens within these inputs, as there are more panels that will use unique tokens.

The following is the instance search query:

```
index=perfmon object="Processor"  | stats count by instance | sort +
instance
```

Fill in the **Search String** as shown in the following screenshot:

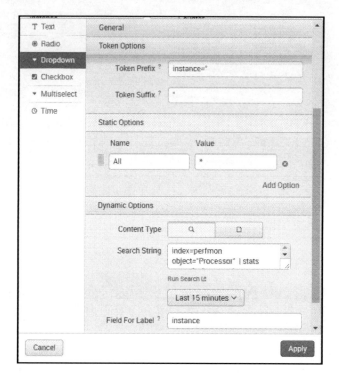

The following is the counter search query:

```
index=perfmon object="Processor"  | stats count by counter| sort + counter
```

Fill in the **Search String** as shown in the following screenshot:

With these in place, we just need to make sure our tokens are labeled correctly, as shown in the following screenshot:

Once we have our tokens labeled appropriately, we adjust our search query in the panel to the search below, and make sure that it abides with the global time range (hist); we then have an identical panel to that in the Windows app. As shown in the following screenshot, it's just powered by individual searches:

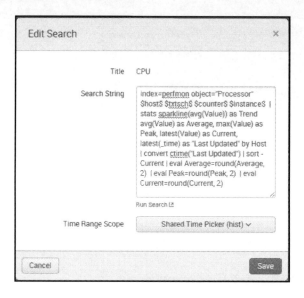

Once we've done a single panel, you can just apply the same technique to all of the other panels within that dashboard, and you will have your own dashboard within your own app.

We can use the same logic and technique to do this with the Linux app in order to get those dashboards in our app.

Search app navigation

With all of the dashboards that you can copy/recreate/consolidate in this way, it can be cumbersome to move around the app and find the right dashboards. Often people go through and look for the name of the right dashboard, but it is much easier to adjust your custom app's navigation XML to accommodate your dashboard. This is an example of a custom app to monitor 12+ systems. Under each of these menus there are around 5+ dashboards that are part of that system, as shown in the following screenshot:

In general, it makes getting around the app and dashboards easier to do.

To adjust this, go to **Settings** | **User Interface** | **Navigation menus** | **yourApp** | **default**.

This should bring you to a screen that looks like XML. The following is an example of the navigation menu to use as a reference for creating your own custom navigation pane. Keep in mind the `view` name is actually the `.xml` file name of your dashboard, and there can be sub menus (sub collections):

```
<nav search_view="search" color="#505153">
  <collection label="OS Overviews">
    <collection label="Windows">
      <view name="sys_win_overview"/>
      <view name="sys_win_web_detail"/>
      <view name="sys_win_host_view"/>
    </collection>
    <collection label="Linux">
      <view name="sys_nix_overview"/>
      <view name="sys_nix_user_detail"/>
      <view name="sys_nix_host_view"/>
      <view name="sys_nix_top_stats"/>
    </collection>
    <collection label="Solaris">
      <view name="sys_solaris_overview"/>
      <view name="sys_solaris_host_details"/>
    </collection>
  </collection>
  <collection label="Cisco UCS">
      <view name="sys_ucs_sytem_summary"/>
      <view name="sys_ucs_lan_overview"/>
      <view name="sys_ucs_fault_overview"/>
  </collection>
  <collection label="Hadoop">
   <view name="sys_nix_hadoop_overview"/>
    <divider/>
    <collection label="Status">
    <view name="sys_nix_hadoop_user_load_nondata"/>
    <view name="sys_nix_hadoop_edge_view"/>
    <view name="sys_nix_hadoop_mapr_cluster_status"/>
    <view name="sys_nix_hadoop_mapr_node_status"/>
    <view name="sys_nix_hadoop_mapr_job_status"/>
    </collection>
    <collection label="Details">
      <view name="sys_nix_hadoop_host_detail"/>
      <view name="sys_nix_hadoop_mapr_job_detail"/>
      <view name="sys_nix_hadoop_mapr_job_history"/>
      <view name="sys_nix_hadoop_yarn_job_list"/>
```

```
      </collection>
      <collection label="Apps">
        <view name="sys_nix_hadoop_compass_summary_view"/>
      </collection>
        <collection label="Leadership">
        <view name="sys_nix_hadoop_user_command_history"/>
      </collection>
    </collection>
    <collection label="Nagios">
      <view name="sys_nix_nagios_alert_monitoring"/>
      <view name="sys_nix_nagios_notification_monitoring"/>
    </collection>
      <collection label="SAS">
      <view name="sys_nix_sas_grid"/>
      <view name="sys_nix_sas_top_stats"/>
      <view name="sys_nix_sas_job_count_by_state"/>
      <view name="sys_nix_sas_heatmaps"/>
      <view name="sys_nix_sas_quick_view"/>
    </collection>
      <collection label="SCOM">
        <view name="sys_win_scom_alert_monitoring"/>
    </collection>
    <collection label="Web Systems">
      <view name="sys_win_web_overview"/>
      <view name="sys_win_web_services"/>
    </collection>
    <collection label="SQL">
      <view name="sys_windows_sql_overview"/>
      <view name="sys_win_sql_database_list"/>
      <view name="sys_win_sql_instances"/>
      <view name="sys_win_sql_missing_indices"/>
      <view name="sys_win_sql_underused_indices"/>
    </collection>
    <collection label="Storage">
      <view name="sys_nix_storage_overview"/>
      <divider/>
      <collection label="EMC">
        <collection label="Summary">
          <view name="sys_nix_storage_emc_cluster_summary"/>
          <view name="sys_nix_storage_emc_volumes_summary"/>
          <view name="sys_nix_storage_emc_initiators_summary"/>
          <view name="sys_nix_storage_emc_targets_summary"/>
        </collection>
        <collection label="Performance">
          <view name="sys_nix_storage_emc_cluster_performance"/>
          <view name="sys_nix_storage_emc_volume_performance"/>
          <view name="sys_nix_storage_emc_initiators_performance"/>
          <view name="sys_nix_storage_emc_target_performance"/>
```

```
            </collection>
        </collection>
        <divider/>
        <view name="sys_nix_storage_emc_events"/>
    </collection>
      <collection label="WAS">
        <view name="sys_win_jvm_was_overview"/>
        <view name="sys_win_jvm_web_details"/>
      </collection>
    <collection label="Statistics">
      <view name="sys_nix_hadoop_mapr_statistics"/>
      <view name="sys_nix_sas_statistics"/>
      <view name="sys_win_statistics"/>
    </collection>
      <view name="reports" />
    <view name="alerts" />
    <view name="dashboards"/>
    <view name="search" default='true'/>
  </nav>
```

Consolidating indexing/forwarding apps

Oftentimes, there is a plausible reason to consolidate apps that either forward data to Splunk or transform data before it is written to disk. This reduces administrative overhead, and allows a single package to be deployed to all systems that spin up with those criteria.

I will use Hadoop for this example. Let's hypothetically say you have 600 nodes in a Hadoop cluster (all on a Linux platform) on which we would also like to monitor CPU, Memory, and disk metrics. Within that Hadoop system, apps such as **Spark** or **Hive** and **Hive2** and **Platfora** each have their own logs and data inputs. Some of these components have Apache web frontends, which will also need to be parsed, but not all nodes will need this.

It takes some magic with the deployment server to make it work, but there is a relatively easy way to do it. We create a consolidated forwarding app (that is, a deployment app) and a consolidated cluster app (that is, an indexing app).

Forwarding apps

These apps generally consist of only a few files, and they are all relevant to sending data to the indexing tier from a universal forwarder. They may have scripts within them too, such as the **Splunk_TA_nix** app. A heavy forwarder can do more things, and can be configured in this way, though for now we will stick to universal forwarders.

File Name	Contents
Inputs.conf	Contains all data input configurations.
Outputs.conf	All relevant data routing configurations, or which indexers /ports to send data to.
Limits.conf	This is only present when the data volume itself coming from a system is excessive. You can adjust features such as data throughput and block size here.

All of these files end up in the /opt/splunk/etc/deployment-apps/<appName>/local folder of your deployment server in order to be distributed to the desired system.

So, taking the preceding example of Hadoop, IIS, and Spark, we create a consolidated inputs.conf file to place in our app.

We can use the inputs.conf of the Splunk_TA_nix app as a starting point, since all of these systems are running on Linux and we want to monitor the CPU, memory, and disk metrics of these machines as well.

When we leverage the knowledge of our Hadoop SME's and get all the log locations for our Hadoop infrastructure, we can simply add those data inputs to the bottom of that inputs.conf file.

We end up with something that looks like the following in our inputs.conf file:

```
### LINUX OS INPUTS
[script://./bin/vmstat.sh]
interval = 60
sourcetype = vmstat
source = vmstat
index = imdos
disabled = 0

### HADOOP INPUTS
[monitor:///opt/mapr/hadoop/hadoop-*/logs/*historyserver*]
```

```
sourcetype = hadoop_historyserver
index = hadoopmon_metrics
disabled = 0

[monitor:///opt/mapr/hadoop/hadoop-*/logs/*nodemanager*]
sourcetype = hadoop_nodemanager
index = hadoopmon_metrics
disabled = 0

[monitor:///opt/mapr/hadoop/hadoop-*/logs/*resourcemanager*]
sourcetype = hadoop_resourcemanager
index = hadoopmon_metrics
disabled = 0


### Web Logs - Apache Tomcat
[monitor:///opt/tomcat/logs/catalina.out]
disabled = 0
sourcetype = hadoop:tomcat:catalina
index = hadoopmon_web

[monitor:///opt/tomcat/logs/localhost.*]
disabled = 0
sourcetype = hadoop:tomcat:app
index = hadoopmon_web
```

I have seen hundreds of data inputs consolidated into a single `inputs.conf` file in this way on a system before. If you use a system such as Puppet or StackIQ, you can configure it to deploy this package whenever a new system within that Hadoop cluster is spun up, and it will report into Splunk, getting the right configurations.

If the data inputs don't exist on that machine then that machine won't send that kind of data, and it has no impact on the functionality of the forwarder sending data.

Usually, with Hadoop, it's ideal to make an app per cluster, as clusters are configured uniquely.

> If you're using Linux, make sure that the user running Splunk owns all the folders and files that you create. If you don't `chown` the new files, they will not be deployed, as the Splunk service doesn't have privileges to touch them. Splunk itself may not even restart on the deployment server.

Indexer/cluster apps

These apps are usually very similar to deployment apps, and they are used to do all pre-index data parsing, or to pull any data from these machines. It's common to use these types of apps to pull **Splunk on Splunk** data from a cluster of indexing peers to write performance metrics of those machines to disk in Splunk.

The important files to note here are:

File Name	Contents
Inputs.conf	Contains all data input configurations.
Outputs.conf	All relevant data on routing configurations, or which indexers /ports to send data to.
Props.conf	Contains all transform calls for source type/index changing, or data rerouting.
Transforms.conf	This has all necessary transformations of the data to be written to disk.

The biggest difference in these apps is their location, depending on your architecture, and the settings within the `props.conf` and `transforms.conf` files. For instance, if you're running a single indexer/search head combo then you have little to worry about, but if you move to indexer clustering it's a bit different. They become cluster apps and must be distributed by the indexing tier cluster master, otherwise they can cause errors with your system.

We will be assuming here that you have dealt/built an indexing cluster, and understand the fundamentals of what that means.

Before creating a cluster app in the `/opt/splunk/etc/deployment-apps` folder on a deployment server and attempting to deploy it to the indexer, or before attempting to install the app directly on the machine in the `/apps` folder... STOP!

These apps can only be placed on the cluster master, in the `/opt/splunk/etc/master_apps` folder. Within that directory you will see a `/_cluster/local` folder, which is where it's best to consolidate everything; however, if you choose to deploy apps to your cluster, you can do so from `/master_apps/`.

These apps are built the same way as the forwarding apps, with settings.

Here is an example of a props/transforms that has consolidated settings for
RSA/DNS/syslog and more in it:

The following is the contents of `Props.conf`:

```
###    RSA SecurID Settings    ###
[rsa:syslog]
TRANSFORMS-runtime = rsa_runtime
TRANSFORMS-system = rsa_system
TRANSFORMS-admin = rsa_admin
LINE_BREAKER = ([\n\r]+)\w{3}\s+\d{2}\s\d{2}:\d{2}:\d{2}\s+
MAX_TIMESTAMP_LOOKAHEAD = 19
SHOULD_LINEMERGE = false
TIME_PREFIX = ^

###    DNS Settings    ###
[MSAD:NT6:DNS]
BREAK_ONLY_BEFORE_DATE = true
TRANSFORMS-filter1 = dns_filter_local
TRANSFORMS-filter2 = dns_filter_internal
TRANSFORMS-filter3 = dns_filter_wpad
TRANSFORMS-fields = answer_section_field

###  Syslog Settings              ###
[syslog_pool]
TRANSFORMS-wips = wips_events
```

The following is the contents of `Transforms.conf`:

```
###    Cisco WIPS Events    ###
[wips_events]
REGEX = WIPS
DEST_KEY = _MetaData:Index
FORMAT = network

###    DNS Event Filtering    ###
[dns_filter_local]
REGEX = \.local
DEST_KEY = queue
FORMAT = nullQueue

[dns_filter_internal]
REGEX = 10\.78
DEST_KEY = queue
FORMAT = nullQueue

[dns_filter_wpad]
REGEX = brq_int
```

```
DEST_KEY = queue
FORMAT = nullQueue
```

Here we can see that we are filtering out some unwanted events in DNS, while extracting other fields and filtering out some things from the syslog pool too.

Summary

In this chapter, we have discussed how to take a series of apps from Splunkbase, as well as any dashboard that the user created, and put them into a Splunk app for ease of use. We have also talked about how to adjust the navigation XML to ease user navigation in such an app. In the next chapter, we will be discussing how to route data sets around an enterprise environment. We will also be discussing leveraging Splunk's data routing capabilities, effectively sending the same data (often OS level metrics such as CPU/disk/memory) to multiple destinations.

10
Advanced Data Routing

Data routing is something that is becoming more common place in an enterprise. As many people are using big data platforms like Splunk to move data around their network things such as firewalls and data stream loss, sourcetype renaming by environment can become administratively expensive. There are some easier ways to get data to another data center or a different environment leveraging only Splunk and some of its more advanced features. We will delve a little deeper into the architecture in this chapter in order to subvert some firewalls, and some license restrictions.

In this chapter, we will learn about:

- Splunk architecture (enterprise level):
    - Clustering
        - Multi-site redundancy
    - Leveraging load balancers (F5)
        - Failover methods
    - Putting it all together
- Network Segments:
    - Production
    - **Standard Integration Testing (SIT)**
    - Quality assurance
    - Development
    - DMZ (a.k.a. App tier)
- The data router:
    - Building roads and maps
    - Building the UF input/output paths
    - Building the HF input/output paths

Splunk architecture

At enterprise level it is rare to deal with a distributed deployment as opposed to a clustered deployment (and depending on the scale of your systems, the cluster and **Disaster Recovery (DR) / High Availability (HA)** components of Splunk will be pretty large). It's usually a good idea to use DNS addresses, hardware load balancing, and clustering (both search tier and indexing tier clusters) in order to meet all of the enterprise level DR/HA policies. In an enterprise level network, there are plenty of security restrictions that won't allow data to flow freely to Splunk from one source or another, and in this case, I am going to attempt to give some insight and an example of what has been used previously and does work in order to distribute data to different environments within an enterprise deployment. There are far too many aspects to Splunk architecture to cover in a single chapter, so I will use those that are relevant to the concept of a data router.

Clustering

Clustering can happen within at least two tiers of the Splunk architecture, one being the search tier, and the other being the indexing tier. These are both important to HA policies, and even though Splunk clustering can be complicated, it is often worth it in order to effect uptime metrics within an enterprise.

Search head clustering

Search head clustering happens with at least three or more search heads and can be setup by the Splunk admin. This is the replacement to Splunk's previously used **search head pooling** which is no longer supported in Splunk 6.3 and above. This type of clustering maintains app and user continuity across the cluster *much* better than the previous pooling method, and is also very similar in administration to that of an indexing cluster. This cluster is managed through the **search head captain** component of Splunk, which is Splunk enterprise, and it is installed and configured slightly differently.

Indexer cluster

This cluster is that of your data stores or indexers, and has the capability to spread data across multiple devices and keep multiple copies. There are two different types of copies in indexing cluster stores, one being the searchable copies and the other being the replicated copies. Both of these affect the amount of HDD space you will need on each device within your indexing cluster. This tier is maintained by the **Cluster Master** component of Splunk, which is also a Splunk enterprise that is installed and configured slightly differently.

Multi-site redundancy

Within the indexing cluster, there is the option to leverage a multi-site redundancy feature within Splunk. This would allow you to have your primary indexers in one site and then replicate the same data to another DR site without it impacting your license. This feature comes in handy when trying to meet both HA and DR requirements of a system within an enterprise without a cost component. This is not an easy feature to implement, as it usually requires a complete overhaul of a Splunk environment. Be cautious when setting this up and it's always best to use test devices first. It's not always possible but testing is definitely a best practice.

Leveraging load balancers

Hardware load balancing in Splunk architecture is absolutely great to have if you can implement it. That is effectively putting something like an F5 device in front of all of your search heads. Using a **Global Traffic Manager** (**GTM**) and **Local Traffic Manager** (**LTM**) device in order to designate appropriate load balancing pools is a great way to increase performance on your search head cluster.

Load balancers can be used for any tier within the Splunk architecture. However, I wouldn't suggest using them for anything other than the search tier. If you apply load balancers to your data streams, you can start confusing the indexers as to where the data is located within the indexes.

Failover methods

With load balancers there is a series of different methods to use. Taking into account that in these examples we will only be using load balancers in front of our search tier, **Round Robin** and **Least Loaded** are the load balancing methods we will be using. Without going into too much detail about load balancing methods/algorithms, let's just stick to these two methods. I will explain these two methods at a very high level. Please do more research to find out the nuances of each of these methods.

Round Robin

Round Robin load balancing is a method in which a device chooses one machine to load balance connections to until it is either full or unavailable, and then routes connections to the next device in the load balancing pool. This is shown in the following diagram:

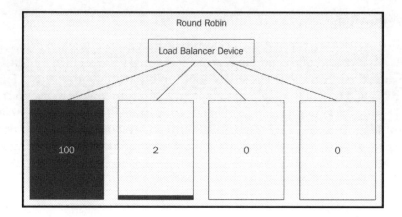

This method is great at GTM level or global load balancer between sites.

Least Loaded

The Least Loaded method is exactly what it sounds like. The load balancing device keeps track of how many connections are active on each device and makes sure that they all remain equal. This is shown in the following diagram:

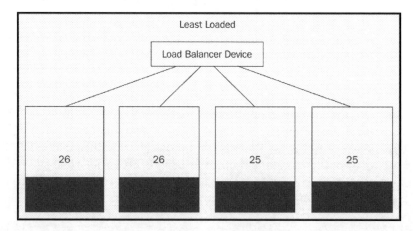

This method is great for the LTM level or the local intra-site level to manage device failover.

Keep in mind that these methods are being summarized greatly, so please suspend your disbelief for this part.

Used in concert, this can help us meet HA/DR requirements.

Putting it all together

When we put search/indexer clusters and load balancers together, we end up with a multi-site redundant DR/HA ready Splunk system that can be leveraged by an entire enterprise.

Our users will hit a Splunk DNS alias, usually something like `splunk.myCompany.com` and that will send their connection to a load balancer, which will then route their connection to the proper search heads, and so on. This is quite a crash course in architecture to help you understand how complicated a single Splunk system can get when it is scaled up to an enterprise level. The nuances come into play when security or governance gets involved between different systems.

Here is a mock-up of a single architecture within a made up enterprise with multiple data centers that requires HA and DR:

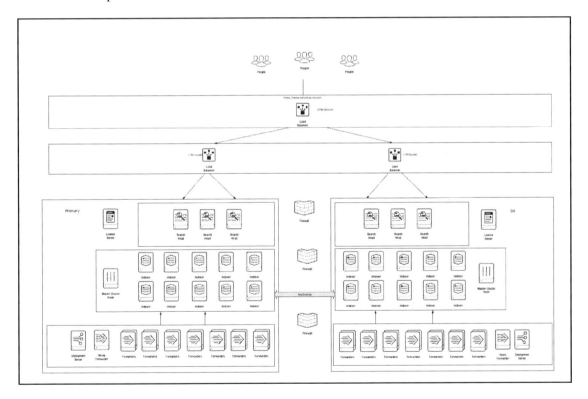

Network segments

To understand the challenges that face us with data routing, we will familiarize ourselves with the different network segments that exist within an enterprise network for the life cycle of software. We will use the idealized version of network segmentation, as this gives us the most complete view, though rarely do all of these exist together at an enterprise. There will be a semblance of these network segments at each enterprise, though due to policies and different cultures, these segments can vary in existence, as well as name. The reason why these are important is because each segment is usually protected by a series of firewall rules. Sometimes these rules can bend, sometimes they can break, other times they are immovable objects. These rules pose challenges to getting Splunk data from the forwarders to the indexers.

For those of you unfamiliar with what a network segment is, a network segment is usually an IP address space, a VLAN, or a series of both that all machines that serve a specific purpose exist on. They are *segmented* from each other so data doesn't end up in the wrong place at the wrong time and cause catastrophe.

Production

This segment is probably the most well-known, as everyone has a *production* environment. This is the network that all application users leverage in order to utilize a service. All of these machines are usually guarded by the strictest of processes in order to maximize user experience and uptime. Basically, this is what your customers are paying to use. This is wrapped in a high level of security in order to protect users from any unexpected impact.

In some companies (more than you'd think), testing in production is common practice. This usually leads to outages and broken dreams because the code hasn't been through any form of testing and is simply rammed into place due to leadership screaming about a deadline. This is bad practice, though not uncommon.

Standard Integration Testing (SIT)

This network segment is where software is released into a production-like environment in order to integrate the new functionality with the old software, so as to ease the user impact. This usually has the exact same components as production, though an enterprise will invite a subset of their users (usually their premier customers) to *test* the functionality of the new software before it is released to production. One could think of this as a kind of *beta testing* environment that customers actually give feedback on in order to resolve any bugs.

This environment is usually firewalled off from any environments above and below in order to make the testing of the new software as secure as possible, and mitigate impact to only the customers who are willing to accept the risks, and provide feedback to the developers.

Quality assurance

This is a network segment that people are paid to break the latest software as much as they can. The environment is a SIT like architecture, though there are no live customers leveraging any of this software. There are only internal staff members using the latest software releases, attempting to break everything they can in order to get the bugs out of the software.

The **Quality assurance (QA)** team reports their findings back to the developer, and the developer will fix all of the bugs that the QA team finds. The purpose is to clean out the software bugs before paying customers actually use the software.

This environment is usually segmented off with a very high level of security due to the amount of people truly attempting to break the software. The actions of the QA team should never reach production, as it is quite literally their job to cause outages in the software, hence the high security rules.

Development

This segment probably has the most names and is the most confusing. Development is also known as staging, testing, dev, or coding, and is often confused with QA (because QA testers often have access here and vice versa). In most organizations I've seen, there are simply two pieces to the development environment, as follows:

- The developer's workstation
- The server(s) they put their new code on to make sure it works

Make no mistake, whatever designation your developers work in, they have almost all access to everything in it, and their personal workstations can connect and administer machines in your development environment. Just substitute development for *<your company lingo>* here.

The development segment is probably the most chaotic segment within a network and will almost always be completely walled off from everything else. Developers usually have free reign in this segment, so they can use all of the tools they need and connect to which resources are necessary in order to develop their software. The kick in the head is when developers come to you (the Splunk admin) and ask to put their logs in for troubleshooting, and you only have a production Splunk instance.

In an enterprise class organization, development and production don't even know each other exist, nor will they ever and there are very tight policies surrounding that rule.

The DMZ (App Tier)

This segment is a little known network segment that usually exists in every enterprise network. The DMZ is also sometimes called the **App Tier** and is a very small window, which is very closely guarded from QA all the way to production. There are very few systems that get authorization to be a part of this segment and this is mostly designed for monitoring.

The App Tier usually has access to all environments except the developer's workstations, and sometimes even those depending on your security and governance rules.

Due to cost efficiency, it is often cost prohibitive to purchase four appliances with all of the licensing and maintenance, and maintain each of those infrastructures separately, one in each of the environments discussed above. Using that logic, purchase a single appliance, the relevant licenses, and poke a hole in the firewall for all necessary devices. Hence what is known as the *DMZ* or *App Tier*.

These are for systems such as Nagios, **System Center Operations Manager (SCOM)**, or Icinga, the **IP address management (IPAM)** system, or your inventory system, and many times, you guessed it, Splunk. Splunk can consolidate monitoring platforms such as solar winds and SCOM, and save a company, in some cases, millions of dollars in licensing. If you tell a VP that Splunk can save them six figures plus in annual licensing, and they don't have to pay anything more than what they have (depending on your Splunk license) they will give you the keys to unlock almost any door.

Sometimes you can poke as many holes as you need to for a Splunk system to work within firewalls, other times you're limited to a handful of machines. It truly depends on your company and the policies they have in place for firewall policies.

The data router

The Splunk *data router* is more of a concept than an actual *thing*. This is basically just a series of heavy forwarders sitting in a global location (preferably a DMZ) that route data to either a single indexer cluster or a series of them depending on your license. I have used the data router successfully in a previous life and it allows developers and security, as well as auditors, a single place to order data from.

I use the word *order* because you can literally make what I call a menu (which is a list of the data types) and allow different departments to pick what data they want. Just be sure to get approval by leadership, for security reasons.

The following diagram is a realistic representation of how the network segments that we spoke of earlier have a relationship with each other:

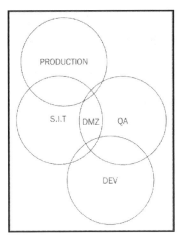

As you can see in the preceding diagram, the DMZ is a great place to put the data router, so we will use this for our example.

Let's assume each of these segments has 200+ forwarders in each of them and we have been tasked with sending all of that firewalled data to a single production Splunk instance. However, one of the many development teams also has a Splunk instance that they maintain and use to centralize logging and troubleshoot their applications.

They would like to see production data within their development Splunk instance, but only for their specific application.

The following are a couple of key requirements to make this a reality:

- Universal index naming
- Data to port mapping

Building roads and maps

Building a data router is as easy as setting up an array of heavy forwarders. The hardest part is the before work, which is creating the data maps and opening the firewalls. There is no quorum to hold on heavy forwarders, so you can have as many as your fault-tolerance requires. In this example, I will use five forwarders as the data router and we will see how to manipulate the data streams within them. We will need to build these forwarders within the DMZ so that all nodes within our environment can send data to them.

We will start with the following high-level diagram of what the data router looks like and its relationship with enterprise data centers:

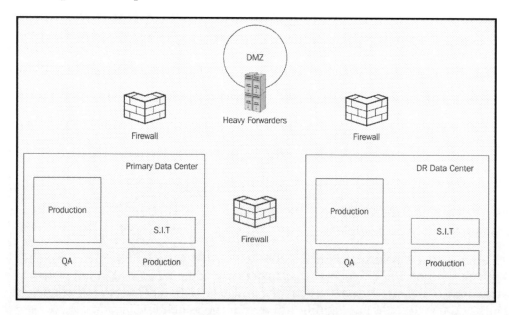

One of the first things we will need to do is open a firewall request to open (arbitrary number here) 100 ports, and in this case, we will use 9900 to 10000. These can be labelled as `splunk ports` and we can wrap an **Access Control List (ACL)** around them.

The next thing we will need to do is start mapping our data inputs to ports within that range. Meaning that Windows (AD) data is on port 9900, Windows events are on 9901,

Linux OS data is on 9901, syslog data is on 9902, and so on.

The following is an example data map for reference that we will be using for this example:

Data set	Data port
Windows events	9900
MS Exchange	9901
Perfmon	9902
MSAD	9903
Linux (OS)	9904
Hadoop (MapR)	9905
Syslog	9906

We will then need to open a firewall request from the heavy forwarders to both sets of indexers (production/development). For our example, we will use the default port to communicate with the indexers (9997), windows perfmon, and Linux OS data. Keep in mind that the destination indexer cluster is responsible for data replication to any other site.

The data flow itself will then look something like the following diagram:

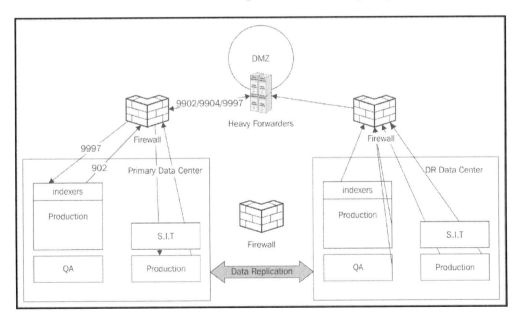

The point of opening the firewall for 100 ports is so that in the future you don't have to open the firewall for any other future datasets, as they can simply be assigned to one of the 100 ports. They can also be replicated to any destination set of indexers. Some companies won't allow the opening of 100 ports, so use your best judgment as to what your security team will allow. Also, the request itself is much less cumbersome, as there are only five machines that need access as opposed to 1000, so it poses much less risk.

Building the UF input/output paths

From a Splunk perspective, we will need to adjust our UF deployment, in order to target the heavy forwarders instead of the indexers. This is done through the `outputs.conf` on your UF. I would recommend using a deployment server for this type of mass configuring. The settings in `outputs.conf` would look something like the following:

```
[tcpout]
forceTimebasedAutoLB = true
autoLB = true
indexAndForward = false

[tcpout:dmz_perfmon]
server = 10.10.10.20:9902, 10.10.10.21:9902, 10.10.10.22:9902,
10.10.10.23:9902, 10.10.10.24:9902

[tcpout:dmz_nix]
server = 10.10.10.20:9904, 10.10.10.21:9904, 10.10.10.22:9904,
10.10.10.23:9904, 10.10.10.24:9904
```

> The `forceTimebasedAutoLB` is an important setting here. Splunk will not normally load balance until the TCP connection is broken. This setting forces the data stream to roll to another forwarder/indexer even if the TCP stream isn't broken. This is necessary so all of your data doesn't end up on a single indexer.

Once you have all of the outputs of your forwarders pointing to your data router, the next step is to begin implementing your data inputs.

Keep in mind that our data inputs are assigned to specific ports within our `outputs.conf` (preceding code) and we will need to call that out with each data input we use.

Let's use a single example of each data type within our `inputs.conf`:

Windows perfmon:

```
[perfmon://CPU]
_TCP_ROUTING = dmz_perfmon
counters = *
disabled = 0
instances = *
interval = 60
object = Processor
useEnglishOnly=true
```

Linux Syslog:

```
[monitor:///var/log/]
_TCP_ROUTING = dmz_nix
whitelist=(messages|secure|auth|mesg$|cron$|acpid$)
blacklist=(lastlog|anaconda\.syslog)
disabled = 0
```

> Notice the _TCP_ROUING = setting in this stanza. This is how we can map
> data sets to different ports, and the HF will accept them on those and
> forward them out how we tell it to.

Building the HF input/output paths

We will need to use the `outputs.conf` and the `inputs.conf` files in order to build this
data router as well, and in these two files the majority of our magic takes place.

When we build these files, we will need to deploy them across all five of our HF's, which
usually means it's easiest to have them connected to a deployment server. I will continue
with the assumption that there is a deployment server configuring the data router.

For the app that is deployed to our data router, we will need to specify all of our indexers
that we want to send data to, and as for the `inputs.conf`, we will need to specify the TCP
port for production as well as our development Splunk instance (or whichever port you've
designated). The settings in `outputs.conf` would look something like the following:

```
[tcpout]
defaultGroup = primaryDC
forceTimebasedAutoLB = true
autoLB = true
indexAndForward = false

[tcpout:primaryDC]
```

```
server = primaryIDX1:9997, primaryIDX2:9997, primaryIDX3:9997,
primaryIDX4:9997, primaryIDX5:9997, primaryIDX7:9997, primaryIDX8:9997,
primaryIDX9:9997, primaryIDX10:9997

[tcpoutput:DRDC]
server = drIDX1:9997, drIDX2:9997, drIDX3:9997, drIDX4:9997, drIDX5:9997,
drIDX6:9997, drIDX7:9997, drIDX8:9997, drIDX9:9997, drIDX10:9997

[tcpoutput:applicationDEV]
server = server1:9997, server2:9997, server3:9997, server4:9997,
server5:9997
```

Here we have a list of our entire Splunk indexer cluster. One for primary, one for DR, and finally the one in the development network segment.

After we create the `outputs.conf` file, we need to have the `inputs.conf` file in all of our Heavy Forwarders be the same.

 It's easiest to package these input/output files in a single app of a deployment server, and then simply update and deploy them to your data router from the deployment server.

When creating `inputs.conf` of our HF, we will leverage the data map that we created earlier and our stanzas within our `outputs.conf`:

```
[tcp://9902]
_TCP_ROUTING = primaryDC,applicationDEV
sourcetype = perfmon
index = perfmon


[tcp://9904]
_TCP_ROUTING = primaryDC,applicationDEV
sourcetype = syslog
index = nix
```

You'll notice that we are using the same `_TCP_ROUTING` method to route data from their respective ports to the destination index clusters.

In an attempt to summarize this section, the following is a diagram, with the correlating configurations:

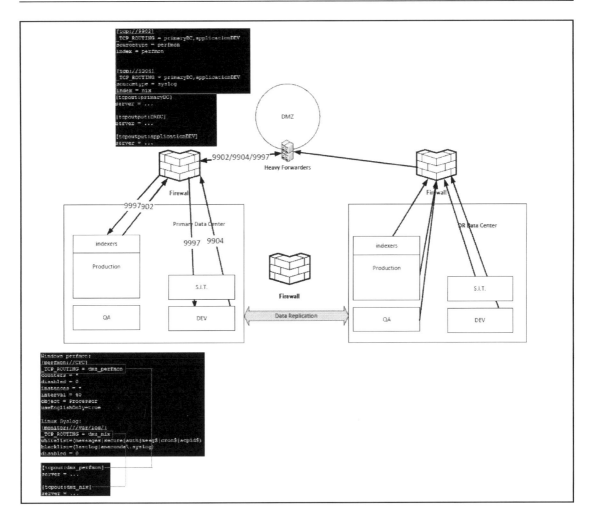

In the preceding diagram, the configurations for the inputs on the forwarder route data to the HF (data router) load balanced and then the data router sends/replicates that data set to both sets of indexers. The cluster master in the production environment is replicating this data to the DR site, so all of your data is now available in three sites.

This architecture can get incredibly complicated depending on how many people are interested in different data sets, as well as what the Splunk team is actually responsible for monitoring and reporting on.

After you get a single instance of this working, you can apply this to any other data set in your universe and replicate or send data to any other Splunk instance in your network, as long as your network team opens a firewall and the license can accommodate the data replication.

This technique can be used in any instance where security is strict and there is a need to limit security vulnerability to a single machine or a handful of machines as opposed to an entire subnet. This can also be handy when working with third-party network vendors, say from a data center, as they will only need to open a handful of addresses as opposed to an entire subnet to allow Splunk data through to your production instance.

If you build it, they will come

No doubt once people understand that you can build a data router, your immediate next step is to track your data map, which will become your menu of sorts. If you choose to market this internally, people will begin to get increasingly curious and specifically if they don't have to purchase a license to test drive their data (which may be as easy as giving them temporary access to an IIS index), word of mouth can start to travel fast.

Make sure to have your processes and policies in place as quickly as you can, because implementing this type of data router into an enterprise class Splunk infrastructure is similar to opening a firehose of possibility into your environment.

I've even known people to charge x dollars for this subset of data and then x dollars for this superset of data subscriptions, which is doable and can affect a departmental budget in a positive way. When licensing is an issue, leveraging this type of methodology or a shared budgeting conversation gets easier.

Summary

In this book, you've been able to learn about some techniques that are moderate and complicated to implement, though all of them can save a Splunk administrator time. Many of these techniques have been used at both small and large companies, as well as enterprise and government facilities from dev-ops to security.

My hope for you is that you glean something that is useful to your day-to-day activities, and leverage it to succeed the way only you know you can. There's a lot of good information within this book, from dashboards, to searching, to advanced data routing, and data model powered panels.

All of these are separate, yet when you pick up these techniques the way you pick up a wrench from a workbench and implement them, you will have many more tools in your belt, to help you look like a rock-star to the next person who asks for the next impossible thing.

There's a lot of assumptions that are made in this book about the skill level of the reader and because of that it may seem like there are things that might look incomplete. The goal here is not to hand you an answer key, but to give you some new information that you can look at and be curious enough about to find out the rest of the information you need to know. We are allowed to be very creative with Splunk to solve some of the most complicated problems that exist in the IT industry today. This won't always be the case, so take advantage while you can!

There is no set path, and there is no paved road for a Splunk journey Splunk is so new and the concept of big data analytics is very fresh. We can either see this as a *new* burden or an opportunity. To me, it's always been a blank slate that we get to discover as we go along. The first time you answer a 15 year old question or resolve a 15 year old problem in a few hours is an amazing feeling and you may not even know how deep of a problem the issue was that you just solved. It will still feel good though.

Everything in this book is open-ended, which to me means take any part of this knowledge or all of it and put your own stamp on it when you apply it. These techniques are not a rule book; they are living methods that you can change to adapt to your circumstances. Everybody's challenges are unique, but with the right tools and enough creativity, we can do some very amazing things.

Index

C

D

logging facility 12

Q

Quality assurance (QA) 211

R

raw data search 164, 166
raw data search panel 164
raw data
  manipulating 73
real-time alerting 105
Recursive Search Post-process 169
REGEX 19
RegExr
  reference 19
report reference panel 164, 172, 174, 176
reports
  about 85
  versus dashboards 146
results, appending in chart
  about 137
  stats 140
  timechart 137
rising column 37
root search 81
Round Robin load balancing 207

S

scripted input 38
search apps, consolidating
  app migratiions 187
  custom app, creating 186
search apps
  consolidating 186
Search Head Captain component 206
search head clustering 206
Search Head Forwarder 36
search modes
  about 127
  Fast Mode 128
  Smart Mode 130
  Verbose Mode 129
Search Processing Language 123
search time data masking 76
search time field extractions

creating 95
sensitive data
  masking 76
Service Now app 42
shared search panel (base search) 164
shared searching
  base search used 168
SharePoint log, with correlation ID
  example 22
Simplified XML 151
single pane of class 186
single-line events
  versus multi-line events 72
Smart Mode 130
SNMP (Simple Network Management Protocol) 41
source type 164
Spark 199
SPL (Splunk Processing Language) 109
Splunk 6.x Dashboard Examples 168
Splunk Answers
  reference 57
Splunk architecture
  about 206
  clustering 206
  leveraging load balancers 207
Splunk deployment server
  about 51, 55
  basic parts 49
  basics 48
  machine specs 49
  reason, for managing data inputs 48
Splunk documentation
  reference 17
Splunk Heavy Forwarder 35
Splunk on Splunk data 202
Splunk search
  anatomy 81
Splunk UI
  event types, creating through 86
Splunk Universal Forwarder 35
Splunk_TA_nix add-on 146
Splunk_TA_nix app 200
Splunk_TA_win
  reference link 188
stats 164